how to create
ROOM
AT THE TOP

Donald R. Brann

FIRST PRINTING — 1978

Published by
DIRECTIONS SIMPLIFIED, INC.

Division of
EASI-BILD PATTERN CO., INC.
Briarcliff Manor, NY 10510

Library of Congress Card No. 77-15691

FIRST PRINTING — 1978

R_x TO BETTER LIVING

With each passing year, houses, like people, face continual change. One may only require minor repair, while others need major operations. Unless repairs are done when conditions dictate, a house loses its capability to provide security, comfort and a long term Capital Gains. Many houses literally begin to shrink as a family grows, while the same size house next door feels big and empty as grown children move out.

Selling a house and buying a larger one formerly provided a logical solution to a space problem. Today, inflated prices, legal and brokers' fees, high moving and decorating costs frequently negate buying a larger house.

A sound and logical approach to creating more living space at a cost every reader can afford is explained in this book. It tells how a pro makes each improvement in words and pictures every reader can follow. Directions cover installation of inside stairs, building a dormer, second story sundeck, modernizing an attic, installing a skylight, converting a second floor into a separate apartment by installing a kitchenette and outside stairs. Every improvement suggested offers privacy for two families under one roof. Equally important, the new housing unit offers an energy saving way to provide shelter for a married or divorced son or daughter at the lowest possible cost. A Supreme Court ruling clarified the right of all members of a family to live under one roof.

Don R. Brann

20375

TABLE OF CONTENTS

7 — How to Create More Living Space

12 — A Safe Way to Work on a Roof

14 — Roofer's Safety Line and Body Harness

17 — Build a Scaffold

19 — Attic Modernization

20 — Tools Needed

22 — How to Build a Dormer

44 — Base and Step Flashing

46 — Fascia, Soffit, Trim

52 — Window Installation

54 — Framing for Air Conditioner

55 — Louver Installation

56 — Build Partitions

63 — Insulation

65 — Application of Wallboard to Ceilings, Walls

69 — How to Build Inside Stairs

82 — Paneling Walls

86 — How to Lay Floor Tile

92 — Hang Doors

93 — Application of Moldings

95 — How to Install a Skylight

105 — A Second Floor Apartment

109 — Installation of an Outside Door

113 — Outside Stair Construction

126 — Sundeck Construction

144 — To Replace a Window

147 — Repairing Damaged Sash

150 — Facts About Glazing

156 — Cross Reference Index to Easi-Bild Books and Patterns

HOW TO CREATE MORE LIVING SPACE

Creating living space is an experience that pays big dividends. What you do in your own home can be done for others. As you read through each page, note each illustration. Keep asking yourself whether you clearly understand each step. If you find directions easy to follow, ask yourself another question. If others can do what the book suggests, why not I?

Doing today what you didn't know how to do yesterday makes life real interesting. How we apply the basic laws of nature helps shape the way we live and our path through life.

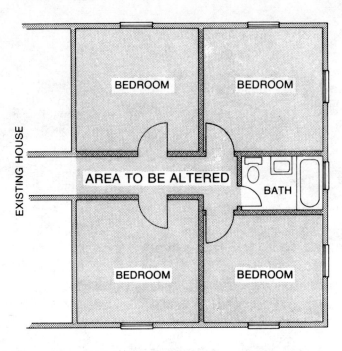

BEDROOM

BEDROOM

AREA TO BE ALTERED

BATH

BEDROOM

BEDROOM

EXISTING HOUSE

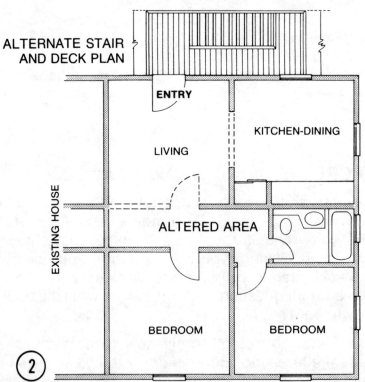

ALTERNATE STAIR
AND DECK PLAN

ENTRY

KITCHEN-DINING

LIVING

ALTERED AREA

EXISTING HOUSE

BEDROOM

BEDROOM

②

Everyone knows heat rises, that even at minimal operational levels a heating unit produces X amount of BTU's. When you apply these two factors to the problem of finding heated living space for a loved one, it's only natural to look up to find the answer.

Homeowners who need additional bedrooms and those with unused ones have a common problem. Both face making a major decision when spendable income is in short supply. Expanding living space in an attic with a dormer, Illus. 1, or converting a second floor into a separate apartment by installing a kitchenette and outside stairs, Illus. 2, permits two families to enjoy the privacy needed with no great increase in the consumption of BTU's. Where there's an artist in the family, directions explain how to install a skylight. Attic studios with a skylight have great income producing potential.

The first step is to decide how much more living space you need, or how much you no longer need. Since a dormer greatly expands space in an attic, it's a sound investment. Its size can best be established by noting how it improves the exterior appearance. Note dormers you find complementary to houses similar to yours and build a comparable size and pitch dormer.

Dash lines, Illus. 3, indicate headroom in an existing attic, while shaded area shows how much more living space can be obtained.

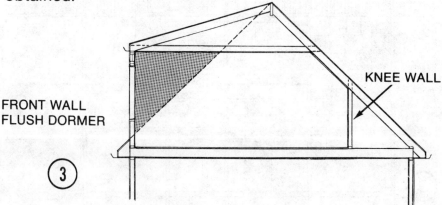

KNEE WALL

FRONT WALL
FLUSH DORMER

3

A shed type dormer is the easiest to build. It can be built flush with the edge of the roof or set back, Illus. 4. Setting a dormer back from edge of roof a distance equal to two or three rafters, greatly simplifies construction. Those who need all possible space should erect dormer flush with the end.

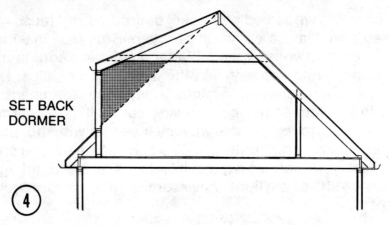

SET BACK
DORMER

④

Depending on your needs and the weather, creating room at the top can begin in any one of several different areas. If your attic is currently accessible by stairs, a start can be made building a dormer. Where an attic is only accessible through a trap door or pulldown stairs, a start can be made building inside stairs. If you are planning a second floor apartment, start by building outside stairs, or a sundeck, Illus. 5, or by cutting an opening for an entry door.

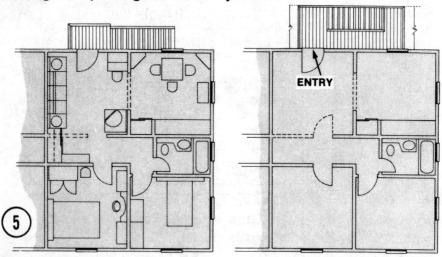

ENTRY

⑤

Attic modernization and dormer construction begin on page 22; installation of a skylight on page 95; construction of inside stairs on page 69;outside stairs on page113;a sundeck on page 126.

In most areas, it's necessary to obtain a building permit to install a dormer, outside stairs, etc. This can be obtained from the assessor's office or building department. Don't file until you become familiar with building procedures.

If this is your first attempt at building, the first reading will naturally seem strange. Even a beginner is agreeably surprised to discover a second or third reading helps to visualize every step. Once construction begins, each progressive step becomes increasingly clearer when a 2 x 4 becomes a shoe, stud, plate or header.

While many will build this dormer entirely on their own, some will hire help. Try to schedule skilled assistance when you can work on the job. By just being around, you gain valuable experience.

Those who wish to buy materials, then hire labor, can still make substantial savings in overall costs. Knowing how the job is done permits shopping intelligently for labor.

When you hire help, you become a contractor. Notify your insurance agent so he can issue whatever temporary insurance he believes will be needed during the period work is being done. Also ask him to check the insurance carried by those you hire. Make certain they carry sufficient insurance to protect you. Don't hire because of price. Make inquiry concerning previous work and try to personally inspect same. If this isn't possible, at least talk to each reference on the phone.

Building is fun. It provides healthy relaxation, exercise and a great feeling of accomplishment. It also provides an economical solution to costly home improvements. But remember, work only when you feel up to it, and only for as long as you feel good. Stop when you get tired, that's when accidents and costly errors occur.

A SAFE WAY TO WORK ON A ROOF

CAUTION: Because of eye or ear trouble, some people should never attempt working on a roof. They just aren't capable of orienting physical activity to height. A dormer installation requires working off a high ladder or scaffold, also on the roof. If you fear working on a roof because you haven't done it before, you can dissipate fear when you follow these steps.

The first and most important step is to learn when and what to do, and how to do it. Working on a roof requires caution, a body harness, roofer's safety line, guts, proper shoes and clothing. Playing safe indicates intelligence. Don't take chances. Don't attempt a job to solve an argument concerning your masculinity or courage. Don't start when you are tired. Don't go up on a roof on a windy day or when it's covered with morning dew or when rain is predicted or the atmosphere is charged with electricity prior to or after a summer storm. Always consider the occupational hazards and take necessary precautions.

Wear high laced, rubber soled, non-skid Keds, Illus. 6. Don't use slip-ons or low shoes. Wear as little loose clothing as weather permits. Wear a roofer's body harness, Illus. 10, and use a roofer's safety line, Illus. 8.

Be sure to disconnect the AC plug to your TV set. Phone the TV serviceman to find out whether your antenna holds an electrical charge. Regardless of what he tells you, don't go near the antenna if the roof is wet, and don't go near if he so advises. If he suggests disconnecting antenna, do so. DON'T WORK CLOSE TO OVERHEAD POWER LINES.

While raising a ladder on soft or sloping ground can be hazardous, it can be done safely if the non-skid base of a ladder is placed on a solid plank, and the ladder is lashed securely to the house. Always anchor a ladder securely at base. Have someone steady it until it can be anchored securely halfway up. If you are working on a two story roof, open a second story window and lash the ladder to a broom handle or 2 x 4 placed across the window frame, Illus. 7. If working between windows, run a line to 2 x 4 across each window.

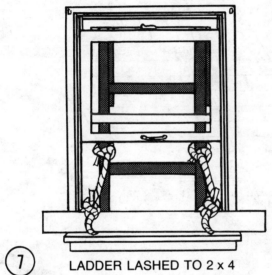

⑦ LADDER LASHED TO 2 x 4

Working on a roof after proper precautions have been taken isn't difficult, and with care it's even safer than crossing many streets. But always remember one basic fact, doing anything for the first time creates a certain amount of fear. This is a normal and natural reaction. Fear is actually a stimulant that sharpens the senses. Consider fear a friendly agent who wants to keep you well and alive.

When necessary safety measures have been taken, and you realize the ladder can't move because it's lashed securely, and you can't fall because you are securely anchored to a safety line, walking and working on a roof loses its danger but still holds its glamour. Being a man is fast becoming a lost art. Don't let it happen to you.

ROOFER'S SAFETY LINE AND BODY HARNESS

A ⅜'' nylon rope, available in most marine supply stores, has a breaking strength of 3400 lbs. To protect the line and shingles on ridge, slide line through a two foot or longer length of discarded garden hose, Illus. 8. To feed line through hose, snake a length of coat hanger wire through hose, press end of wire over rope, Illus. 9, and pull rope through hose.

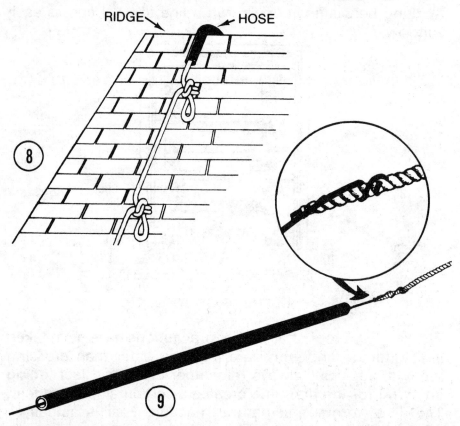

RIDGE — HOSE

Tie one end of safety line to a tree, if convenient; or to a length of 2 x 4 or broom handle, placed across a window or door, Illus. 7.

Use sufficient length for the safety line so you can make 3'' loops every three feet, on side of roof you are working on, and still be able to work all over the roof. Always have someone take up slack after you have achieved working position and anchor free end to a 2 x 4 across inside of window.

14

The safe and smart way to work on a roof is to use a rope body harness, Illus. 10. These are available readymade at marine supply stores, through mail order, or you can easily make one using ⅜" nylon line.

Cut a 39" length of ⅜" line. Using nylon thread, wrap line 4" from each end X, Illus. 11. Separate three 4" long strands. Seal ends with a match flame.

Splice line making a 15" neck halter, Illus. 12. If you can't splice, tie a knot.

Put on clothes you will be wearing while working on roof. Measure your chest girth, multiply by two and add 10". Cut another line to this length.

4" from each end, wrap line with nylon thread. Separate strands, apply flame to ends. Splice ends to fashion a loop, Illus. 13.

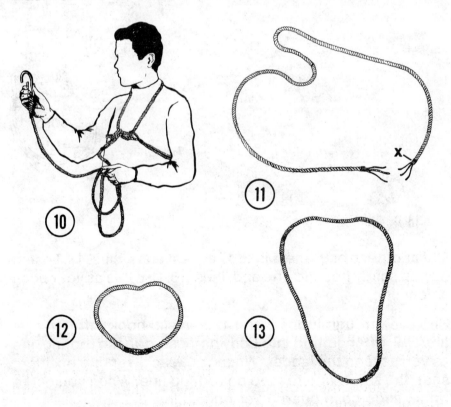

Place big loop through small loop, Illus. 14. Place in position shown, Illus. 15. Wrap with nylon thread at G and H, Illus. 16.

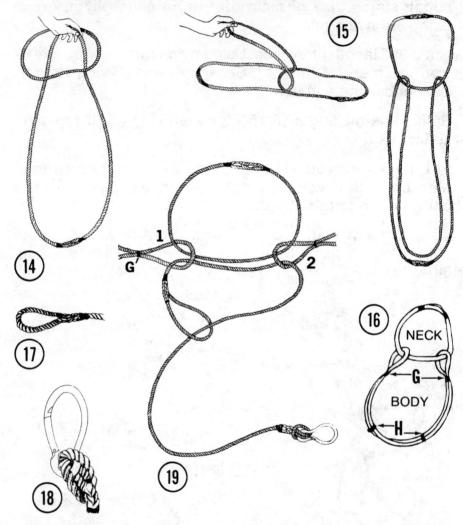

Cut another 6 or 8' line. Make 4" eyes at ends, Illus. 17. Fasten a snap safety hook to one end, Illus. 18. Use this as your body safety line.

Slip eye through loops 2 and 1, then slip hook through eye, Illus. 19. After getting into body harness, grip the roofing line as you ascend the ladder. When you reach working position, snap the safety line to loop on roofing line. When you get to ridge, slide hose guard over ridge, Illus. 8.

BUILD OR RENT A SCAFFOLD

To protect yourself, the roof and gutters, and to simplify handling materials, most professionals work from a scaffold, rather than a ladder. A scaffold simplifies working on a roof. Illus. 20 shows a popular type that can be rented.

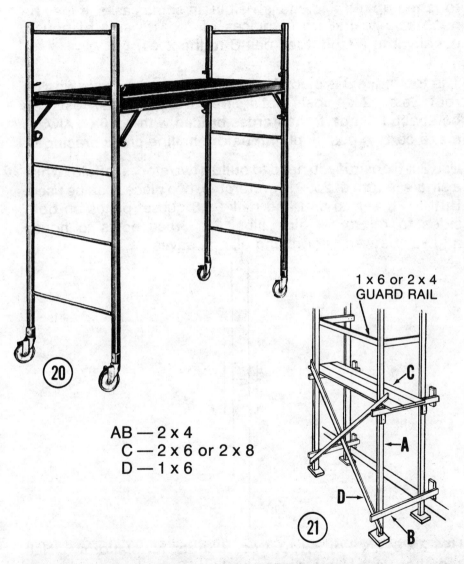

1 x 6 or 2 x 4
GUARD RAIL

AB — 2 x 4
C — 2 x 6 or 2 x 8
D — 1 x 6

Illus. 21 shows a build it yourself scaffold. Use 2 x 4 posts A. If posts need to be placed on soft earth, toenail legs A to short pieces of 2 x 4 or 2 x 6.

17

Place outside posts A about three feet from house. Fasten in place with 1 x 6 or 2 x 4 cross braces B nailed to house. Use level to plumb post. Use 8 penny finishing nails to drive nails into a casing around a window, door, corner trim or siding. Drive nails in securely, but don't drive them home. When removing scaffold, pull nails, fill holes with putty. When touched up, no damage is visible. In some cases, it may be necessary to nail short pieces of 2 x 4 to side of house, usually into a stud, then nail B to the 2 x 4.

The top brace B is placed at a height that permits walking on roof. Select 2 x 4 posts that are free of loose knots. Posts can be spaced 8' apart, then cross braced with 1 x 6 D. Always make certain post is plumb before nailing cross bracing D.

Use 2 x 6 posts if you need to build a two story scaffold. While a single length of 2 x 6 is preferable, two pieces can be used. Butt 2 x 6 end-to-end and nail 1 x 6 gusset plates on both sides to reinforce joint, Illus. 22. Brace posts to house midway between floors and also at eaves.

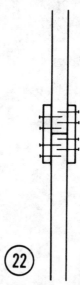

Use 2 x 6, 2 x 8 or 2 x 10, free of knots, for platform C. Nail together with cleats across bottom. Butt cleats against B.

If you rent a scaffold, use it according to directions provided by dealer.

ATTIC MODERNIZATION

Creating an apartment at the top follows this general procedure:

1. Clean out attic.
2. Install inside stairs if required.
3. Nail ⅝ or ¾'' x 4 x 8' plywood temporarily to joists if subflooring is required. If existing stairs prohibit moving 4 x 8 panels, use 4 x 4 or 1 x 6 half lap sheathing boards, Illus. 23, for flooring. Select lumber with no loose knots.
4. Build dormer if same is desired.
5. Frame for window or skylight.
6. Nail ceiling joists.
7. Build partitions.
8. Rough in wiring, plumbing, TV antenna lead-in, telephone line.
9. Install insulation.
10. Nail plywood subflooring.
11. Install gypsum board ceiling.
12. Apply paneling.
13. Lay vinyl or other floor tile or carpeting.
14. Hang doors.
15. Trim doors, windows, base and ceiling.

Those who need to build inside stairs will find directions on page 69.

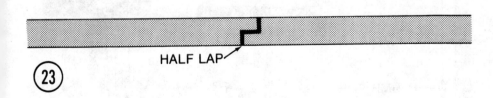

HALF LAP

㉓

TOOLS NEEDED

Besides a hammer, cross cut and rip saw, or better still an electric circular and saber saw, you will need a square, bevel square, chalk line, level, plumb bob, brace and bit or electric drill, Illus. 24.

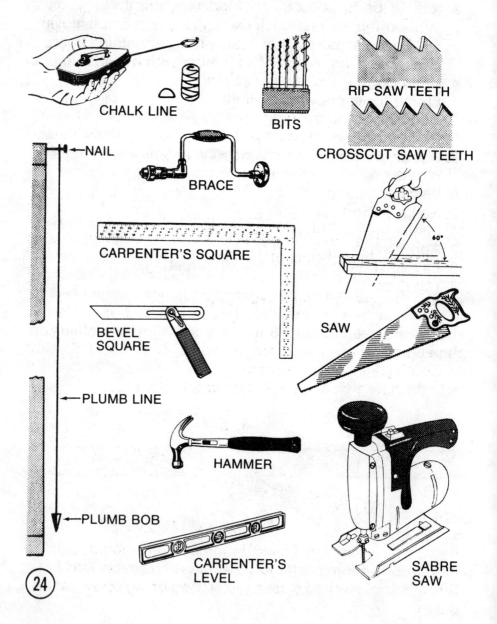

CHALK LINE

BITS

RIP SAW TEETH

CROSSCUT SAW TEETH

NAIL

BRACE

CARPENTER'S SQUARE

60°

BEVEL SQUARE

SAW

PLUMB LINE

HAMMER

PLUMB BOB

CARPENTER'S LEVEL

SABRE SAW

24

BASIC FACTS TO CONSIDER

Prior to getting started, decide what burglary and fire alarm, outdoor floodlighting, air conditioning, stereo, intercom or other equipment you want to install. All wiring should be roughed in prior to applying insulation and paneling.

If the converted space is to be occupied by a musician or music lover, consider the value of soundproofing by applying 3 to 6" of rock wool or rigid foam insulation between floor and ceiling joists. This will help deaden transmission of sound.

If existing stairs or opening in ceiling doesn't permit moving 4 x 8' plywood and gypsum panels into attic, plan on hauling these up when you cut opening for a stairway or dormer. Cover panels with polyethylene to protect against dirt and dampness.

CAUTION: Through the years, many houses were constructed with 2 x 6 ceiling joists. This was sufficient to pass building codes in effect at the time, and to support a plaster or gypsum board ceiling. 2 x 6 is still acceptable as a floor joist on a short span, but could be too light when used for living space in a longer span. To strengthen joists, carefully nail or bolt an extra 2 x 6 to every joist or every other one depending on local code requirements. Additional stiffening to existing joists can be achieved by nailing joists to 2 x 6 cats (bridging) spaced 4'0" on centers, Illus. 25.

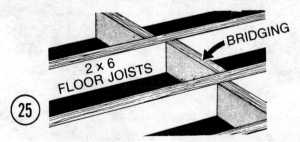

If plaster on ceiling below is loose, don't compound the negative by nailing extra joists or cats in position. Drill holes through the new and existing joist. Bolt or lag screw same in place.

HOW TO BUILD A DORMER

Illus. 26 indicates position of framing required for a dormer. Buy materials as needed. You can reuse existing rafters or buy same size lumber. 2 x 6 ceiling joists can be used for unsupported spans up to ten feet; 2 x 8 for spans over ten feet. Use 2 x 4 for studs, plate, shoe and headers. Use ¾'' plywood for roof and sidewall sheathing. Apply roofing shingles, siding, fascia and moldings to match those on house.

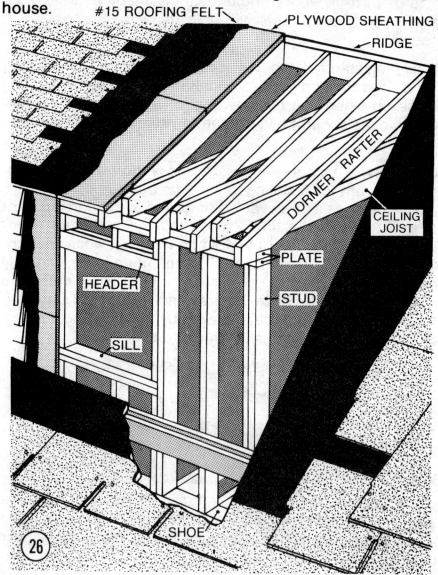

#15 ROOFING FELT

PLYWOOD SHEATHING

RIDGE

DORMER RAFTER

CEILING JOIST

PLATE

HEADER

STUD

SILL

SHOE

26

Many building codes require a minimum 8'0" ceiling height for living space. 7'6" and 7'0" provide usable living space in an attic and same is acceptable in many areas.

Measure distance A from subflooring to bottom of ridge, Illus. 27. Draw same length line down middle of attic. This is line B.

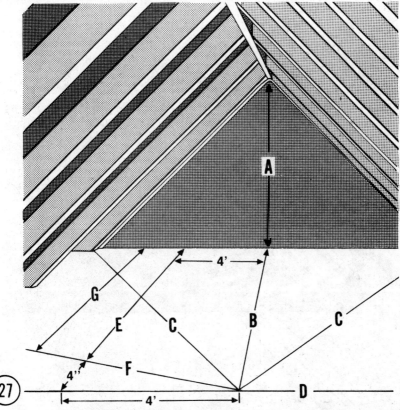

Draw line C to inside edge of rafter. Draw line D at right angle to B. Snap chalk lines.

The minimum pitch of a dormer roof should be one inch to one foot of rafter. To establish this, measure 4'0" from B. Snap a parallel line E.

Measure 4" down E from D and snap line F. This line now represents a rafter having a pitch of 1" = 1'. Line F also indicates amount of headroom a dormer can provide if dormer rafters are cut to angle shown.

Snap chalk line G where it provides usable headroom. G will also indicate inside edge of framing. An easy way to establish angle for dormer rafters is shown in Illus. 28. Place 2 x 4's on lines F and G. With square placed on line B, draw line across 2 x 4. Cut ridge end to this angle. Cut fascia end to dotted line.

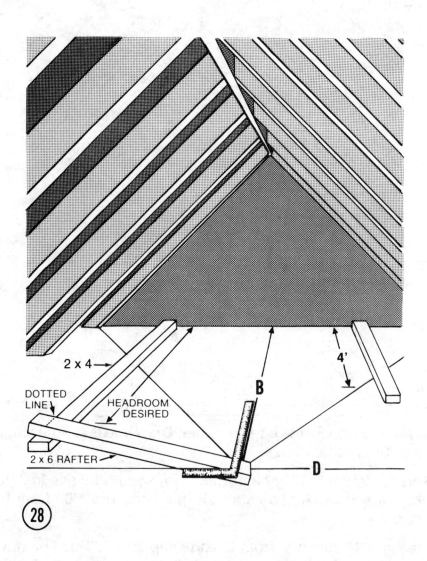

While the roof on house, Illus. 29, has a 12 on 12 pitch, the proposed dormer, shown by dash lines, has a pitch of 5 on 12. This can be covered with shingles.

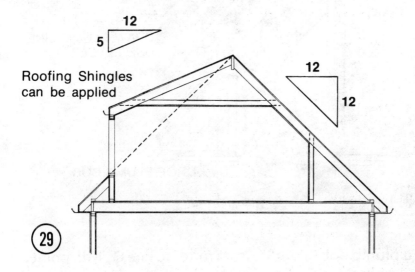

Illus. 30 indicates a dormer with a roof pitch of 3½ on 12. This requires built up roofing.

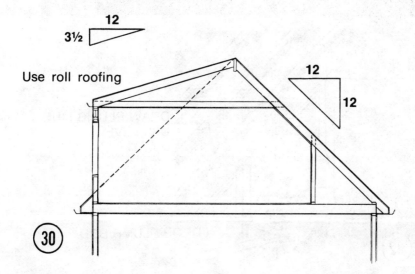

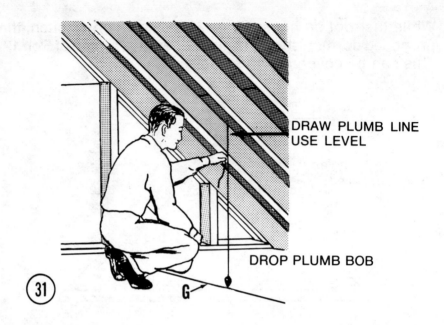

DRAW PLUMB LINE
USE LEVEL

DROP PLUMB BOB

G

③

Drop a plumb bob, Illus. 31, from rafter to line G. With point of bob touching line G, draw line on rafter. Use a level to plumb line. Consider line G as the inside edge of wall frame.

To allow for double header and front wall, Illus. 32, measure over 6⅞" from G and snap line H on floor.

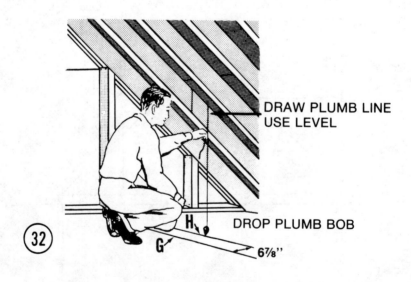

DRAW PLUMB LINE
USE LEVEL

H

DROP PLUMB BOB

G

6⅞"

㉜

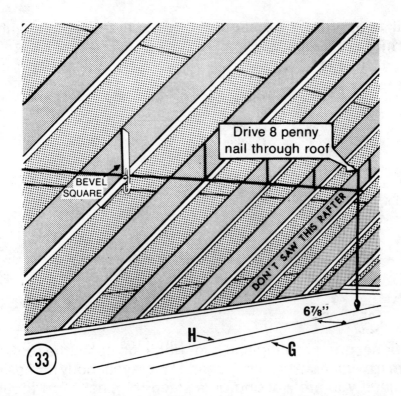

Use the plumb bob to mark line H on end rafters. Use level to plumb line on rafter. Snap a chalk line across all rafters to indicate line H. Set a bevel square, Illus. 33, to exact angle and draw line H on each rafter. Drive a nail through roof on line H at the second or third rafter from each end, Illus. 34.

Nail temporary 2 x 4 supports to ridge and rafters within dormer area, Illus. 35.

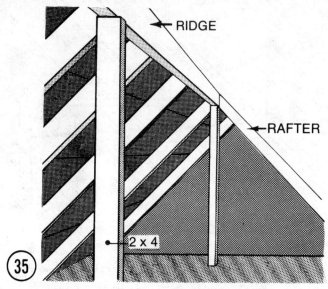

RIDGE

←RAFTER

2 x 4

35

After securing roofing line over ridge, go up on the roof. Be sure to wear non-skid shoes and to have your body harness in place. If you are working on a steep roof, nail 2 x 4 footing scaffolds three feet apart, Illus. 36. Don't drive nails all the way. When you remove these, plug nail holes with asphalt cement.

FOOTING   SCAFFOLD

36

Prior to opening up roof, consider the size, number and placement of windows the dormer will need, Illus. 1. These should match and be positioned over those on lower floors.

Nail a 2 x 4 across rafters, 6" below line H, Illus. 37. Cut 2 x 4 braces to angle and length required. Toenail these in position.

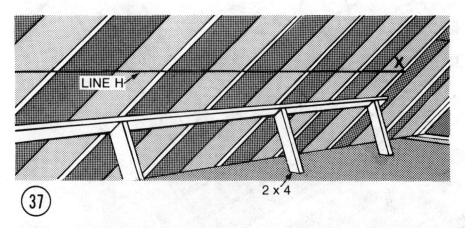

LINE H

2 x 4

(37)

When you have assembled materials needed, plus a canvas or heavy gauge polyethylene of sufficient size to cover opening at night, the next step is to remove shingles and sheathing within area selected for dormer, Illus. 34. To locate exact area, tie a line to nails protruding through roof. Measure distance from nail to gable end, Illus. 38. Mark same distance on ridge. Draw lines. This line should indicate inside edge of either the second or third rafter from end X, Illus. 37.

Start removing shingles at ridge and work your way down. Pry up shingles carefully. If done with care many can be reused. Remove shingles within area of dormer roof plus one full shingle to each side. Remove roofing felt.

If you have an electric saw, saw sheathing flush with dormer side of rafter X. If you use a hand saw, drill hole and start sawing with a compass saw, Illus. 39.

Remove sheathing. Remove nails and place sheathing on floor of attic. Don't drop any lumber or plywood as you could damage plaster in ceiling below.

After sheathing has been removed, saw rafters within area of dormer along line H, Illus. 33. Pry rafters off ridge. Remove nails, place on floor of attic.

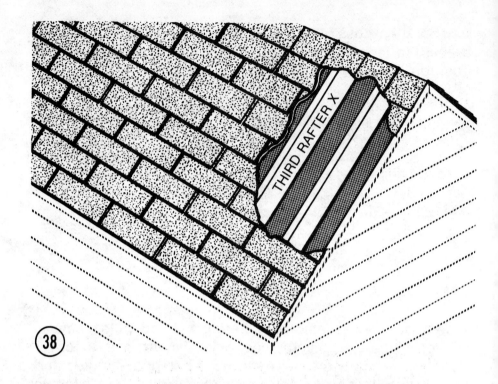

THIRD RAFTER X

(38)

Cut only
exposed rafters

CANVAS or
PLASTIC SHEETING

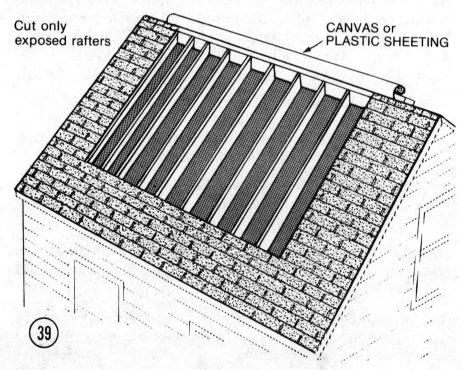

(39)

Now is the time to haul 4 x 8' plywood and gypsum panels into attic.

Nail headers H, Illus. 40, in position. Use lumber one size larger than rafter. If rafter is 2 x 6, use 2 x 8 for H. Nail one header flush with top edge of rafter. Drive two 16 penny nails into each rafter. If two or more lengths of header are required, butt ends together over center of rafter. Nail through end rafter into end of header with two 16 penny nails.

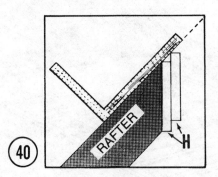

Keep top edge of DOUBLE HEADER "H" in line with rafter

Nail second header H in position shown. If two or more pieces are used for this header, butt ends together so they overlap the joint in the first header by at least two feet, Illus. 41.

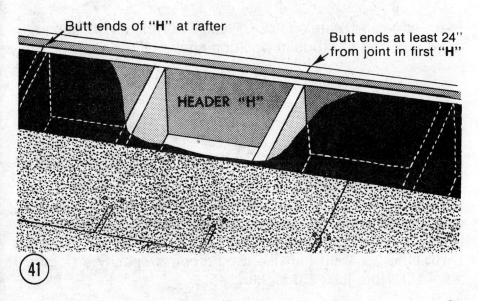

Butt ends of "H" at rafter

Butt ends at least 24" from joint in first "H"

HEADER "H"

Assemble front frame on floor, Illus. 42. Cut studs to length of G less 4½". Cut 2 x 4 shoe and two 2 x 4 plates to length of header H.

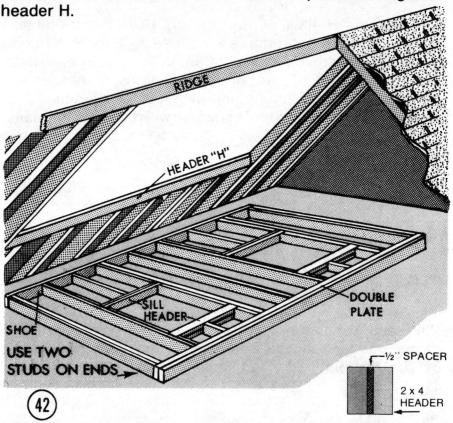

RIDGE

HEADER "H"

SILL
HEADER

SHOE

USE TWO
STUDS ON ENDS

DOUBLE
PLATE

42

½" SPACER

2 x 4
HEADER

Place shoe and plate on floor. Place ends flush. With square, draw location of studs in position shown, Illus. 43.

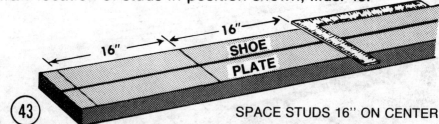

16"

16"

SHOE

PLATE

43

SPACE STUDS 16" ON CENTER

Nail shoe and single plate to studs with two 16 penny nails at each joint. Frame openings for windows to rough opening size retailer suggests. Use double 2 x 4 on edge with pieces of ½ x 3½ x 4" plywood as spacers for headers. Use a single or double 2 x 4 sill flatwise. Some codes specify a double 2 x 4 sill. Note jack studs, Illus. 45.

Measure diagonals, Illus. 44. Frame is considered square when diagonals are equal length. Hit frame at corner to square up. Nail a 1 x 4 or 1 x 6 diagonally across frame to hold it square. Spike second plate in position, Illus. 42.

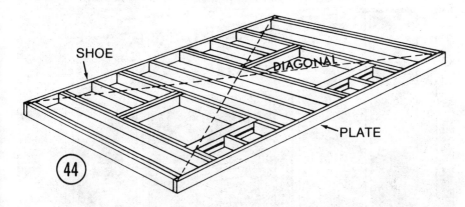

SHOE

DIAGONAL

PLATE

44

Set frame in position, Illus. 45. Plumb with level in two directions. Level frame. Shim under shoe with shingle if necessary.

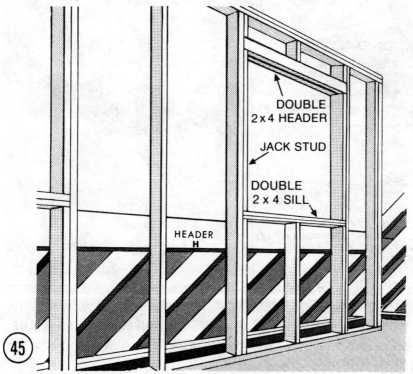

DOUBLE
2 x 4 HEADER

JACK STUD

DOUBLE
2 x 4 SILL

HEADER
H

45

Brace frame in plumb position with 1 x 6, Illus. 46. Nail through shoe into floor joists with 16 penny nails. Nail rafter to end studs. Toenail studs to header H.

Cut ceiling joists, Illus. 47. A considerable saving of material can be effected by cutting two ceiling joists out of the same length of lumber.

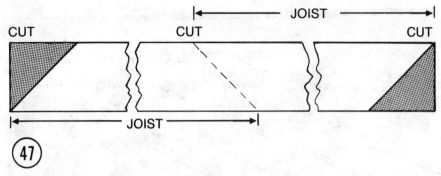

To cut end of joist to angle needed, butt and tack a piece of 1 x 6 against roof sheathing, Illus. 48. Place level on 1 x 6, Illus. 49. When bubble is centered, draw a line. Remove and saw 1 x 6 along this line. This angle can now be used as a pattern to cut end of 2 x 6 ceiling joist, Illus. 50. Place angle end against sheathing on roof, Illus. 51. Cut joists to length needed to finish flush with framing.

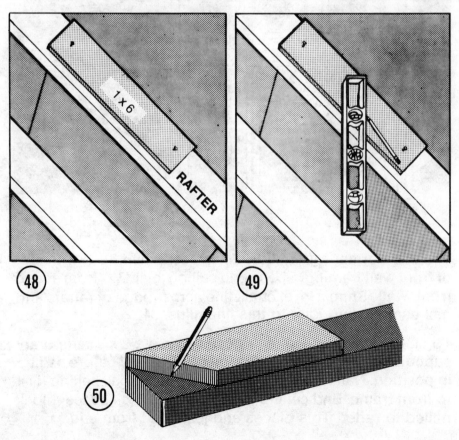

(51)

CEILING JOIST

The end dormer rafter, Illus. 26, is positioned flush with end of front wall framing. Space end ceiling joist 1½'' from end of front wall. Snap a level chalk line across edge of rafters and nail each ceiling joist to this line, Illus. 31.

To simplify nailing joists in position, use a 2 x 4 temporary support, Illus. 52. Check each joist with a level before nailing in position. Nail through joist into rafter. Toenail ceiling joist to front frame. End ceiling joists require a 2 x 4 spacer block nailed to rafter. This places end joist 1½'' from end.

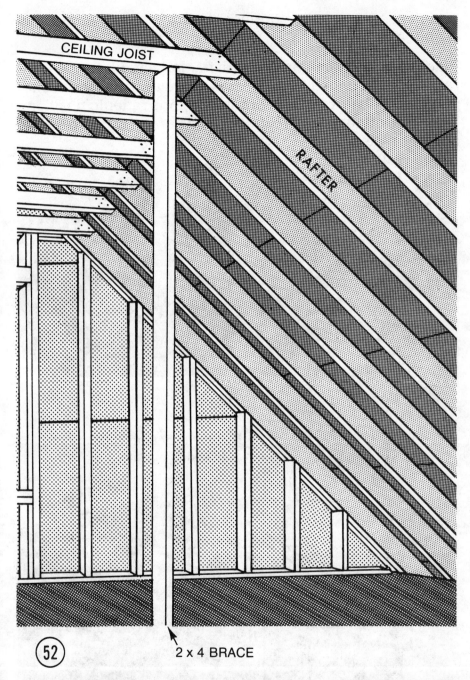

CEILING JOIST

RAFTER

(52)   2 x 4 BRACE

When ceiling joists have been securely nailed in position, temporarily tack 2 x 6's across top of joists. This permits using joists as a scaffold. Remove front wall bracing.

The next step is to cut dormer rafters to length and angle required.

Place a rafter in position on top of frame, Illus. 53. Tack end of rafter to ridge with a 1 x 2, Illus. 54. Drive an 8 penny nail into end of top plate so it temporarily supports rafter in position, Illus. 55. Bottom edge of rafter should be level with top inside edge of plate.

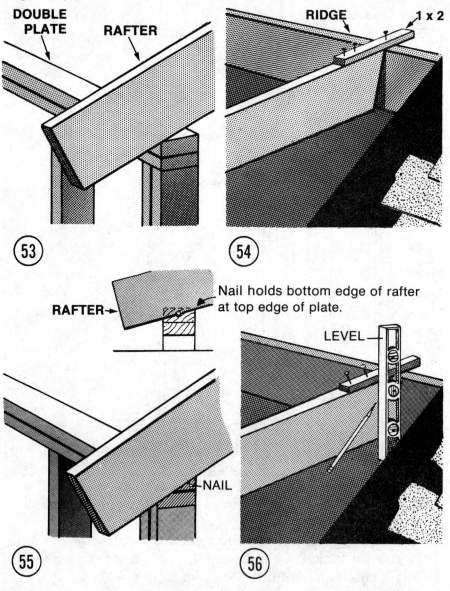

DOUBLE PLATE   RAFTER

RIDGE   1 x 2

(53)   (54)

RAFTER→

Nail holds bottom edge of rafter at top edge of plate.

LEVEL

NAIL

(55)   (56)

Plumb level against ridge and mark rafter, Illus. 56. Remove rafter and saw to angle of drawn line. Place rafter back in position, Illus. 57. Hold in position with 1 x 2.

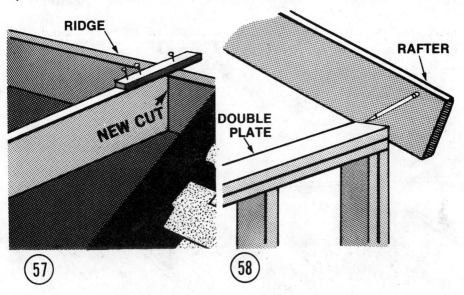

With the nail holding bottom of rafter level with top inside edge of plate, draw outline of plate on rafter, Illus. 58.

Remove rafter. Saw notch. Allow rafter to overhang 6⅜" as shown, Illus. 59. Use level to plumb line. Saw end to length and shape shown.

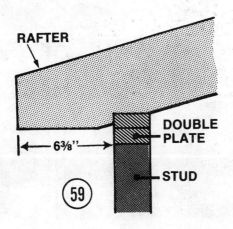

Use first rafter as a pattern, Illus. 60. Nail 1 x 2 blocks as stops.

CUT

CEILING JOIST

16"

Mark and saw other rafters. Toenail rafters to ridge and plate with 8 penny nails. Spike ceiling joists to rafters with 16 penny nails. Chop or saw projecting top end of ceiling joists, Illus. 61, flush with top edge of rafter.

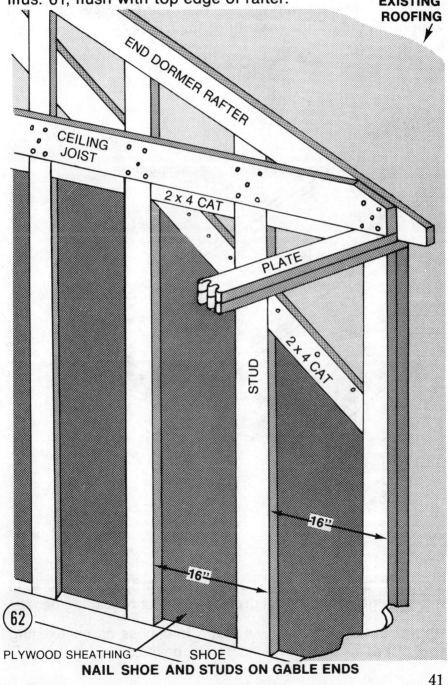

EXISTING ROOFING

END DORMER RAFTER

CEILING JOIST

2 x 4 CAT

PLATE

2 x 4 CAT

STUD

16"

16"

(62)

PLYWOOD SHEATHING

SHOE

NAIL SHOE AND STUDS ON GABLE ENDS

The next step is to stud up gable end with 2 x 4's cut to length and angle required. Nail in position shown, Illus. 62. Nail 2 x 4 cats between studs and rafters, Illus. 62, 63.

Sheath gable ends with ⅝ or ¾" plywood. Saw plywood flush with rafters. Saw front sheathing flush with top of plate, Illus. 63.

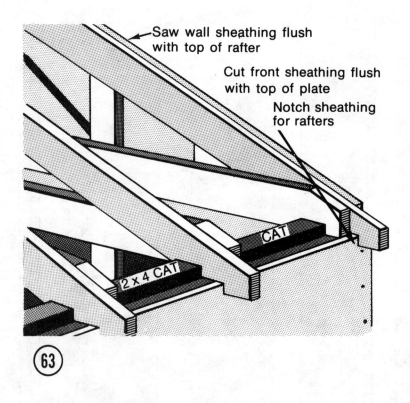

Saw wall sheathing flush with top of rafter

Cut front sheathing flush with top of plate

Notch sheathing for rafters

CAT

2 x 4 CAT

(63)

Cut and nail 2 x 4 cats, Illus. 63. Cats project 1½" beyond inside edge of plate. This provides a nailor for ceiling panels.

Apply roof sheathing. Use same thickness as on existing roof. Roof sheathing projects ⅜" beyond side sheathing.

Staple #15 roofing felt to gable ends, front and roof. Use stapling gun or big head nails. Allow roofing felt to overlap gable ends 4".

Nail ⅜ x 4" lath strips 16" on centers to gable ends, Illus. 64.

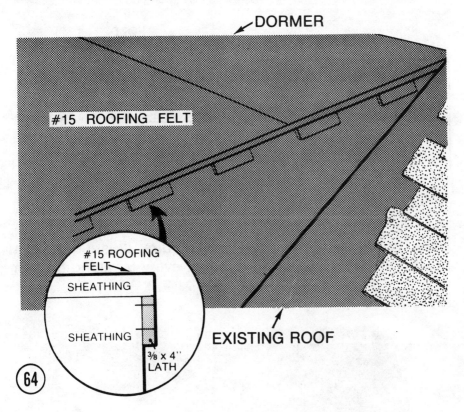

If gutter brackets are to be nailed to roof, space and nail brackets after applying felt. If brackets are to be nailed to fascia, do so after applying fascia.

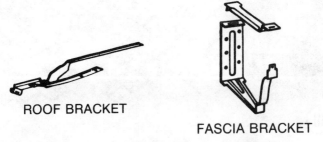

BASE AND STEP FLASHING

Cut an 8 or 10", or width needed strip of copper or aluminum flashing, Illus. 65, to length of dormer, plus 6 or 10". Make a 3 or 5" cut at each end, in position required.

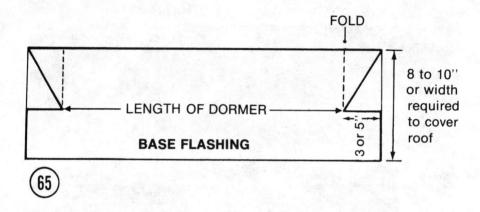

FOLD

LENGTH OF DORMER

BASE FLASHING

3 or 5"

8 to 10" or width required to cover roof

65

Bend to shape dormer and roof require, Illus. 66. Nail in position every 12" along top edge, every 6" along bottom edge.

BASE FLASHING

66

44

Cut and bend an 8 or 10 x 7" piece of flashing for corner, Illus. 67. After applying shingles to the course just below bottom of dormer, apply base flashing. Some builders apply shingles up to base of dormer and expose base flashing. Others apply base flashing, then embed last course of shingles in asphalt cement. Always nail shingles below flashing so no nails penetrate flashing.

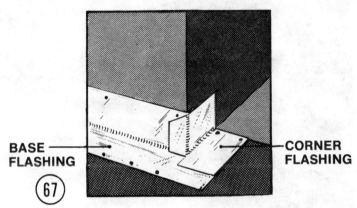

BASE FLASHING

CORNER FLASHING

(67)

Apply step flashing before each course of shingles. Nail step flashing with two nails in position shown, Illus. 68. Step flashing overlaps 2" on vertical joints. Don't drive any shingle nails through step or base flashing.

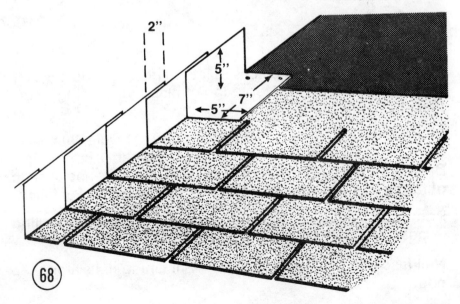

2"

5"

7"

5"

(68)

FASCIA, SOFFIT, TRIM

Use 1 x 6 or 5/4 x 6 fascia on gable ends. To cut fascia to angle and length required, place it in position indicated, Illus. 69. Place a level or length of 1 x 4 on roof. Draw angle at ridge end. Remove fascia. Redraw same angle closer to end. Saw end.

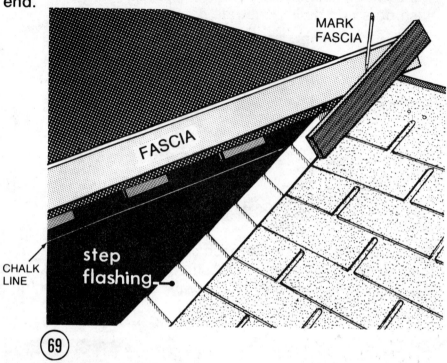

MARK FASCIA

FASCIA

CHALK LINE

step flashing

69

Be sure to nail ⅜ x 4" pieces of lath in position, Illus. 64, 69. These permit inserting top edge of clapboard siding under fascia.

Place a piece of ⅜" lath under ridge end of fascia, flush with edge of roof, Illus. 70. Nail fascia temporarily in position. Draw outline of rafter on fascia, Illus. 71. Remove and cut end of fascia to angle required. Remove lath under end of fascia.

Prime coat fascia and exterior trim with primer before nailing in position.

Nail fascia in position with 8 penny finishing nails along top edge.

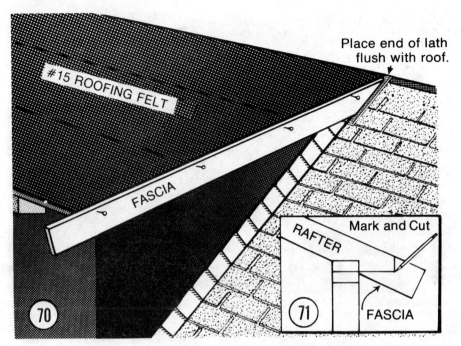

Place end of lath flush with roof.

#15 ROOFING FELT

FASCIA

RAFTER

Mark and Cut

FASCIA

70

71

Cut and nail 5/4 x 8 or 1 x 8 soffit, Illus. 72, flush with end of rafter. Use 8 penny galvanized or aluminum nails. If two or more lengths of soffit are required, butt ends over center of rafter.

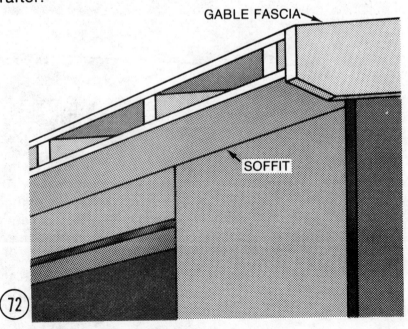

GABLE FASCIA

SOFFIT

72

47

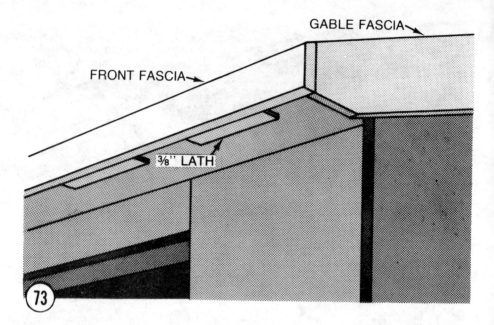

FRONT FASCIA→

GABLE FASCIA↘

⅜" LATH

73

Allow bottom edge of front fascia to project ⅜" below soffit. Temporarily tack ⅜" lath to soffit. Nail gable fascia in position so bottom edge is flush with lath, Illus. 73. Remove lath.

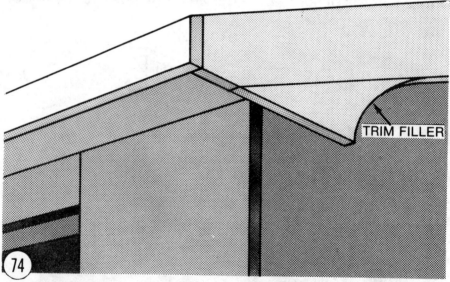

TRIM FILLER

74

Nail front fascia to ends of rafter. Nail front fascia to fascia on gable ends. An alternate gable fascia can be cut to shape shown, Illus. 74, 75. Apply glue to top edge and nail in place.

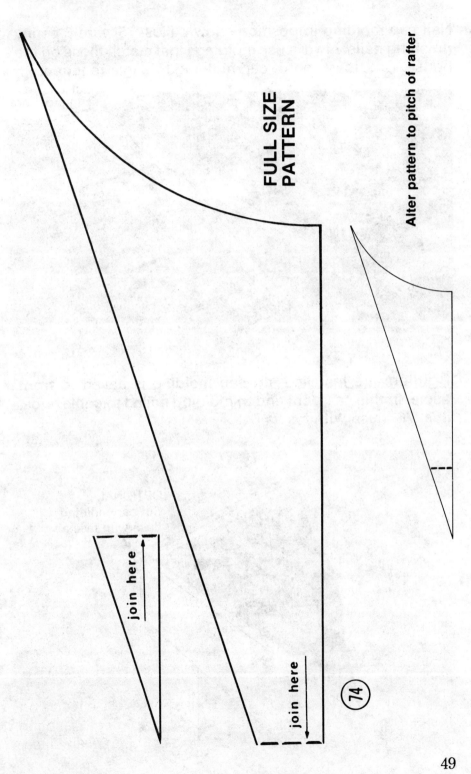

FULL SIZE
PATTERN

Alter pattern to pitch of rafter

join here

join here

74

49

Nail cap molding in position shown, Illus. 75, with 6 penny finishing nails. Always use moldings that match those on the house. Cut ridge end of cap molding to angle required.

Cut end to
angle of roof

75

If gutters are installed, no cap molding is nailed to front fascia. In this case, cut end of molding nailed to gable ends, Illus. 76, flush with fascia.

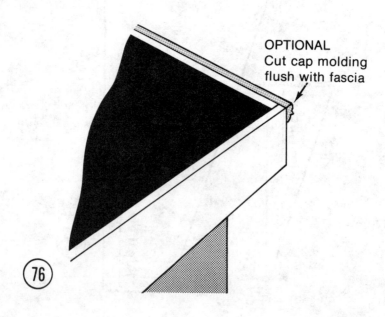

OPTIONAL
Cut cap molding
flush with fascia

76

When no gutter is installed, miter cut molding, Illus. 77, and nail molding across front fascia, Illus. 78.

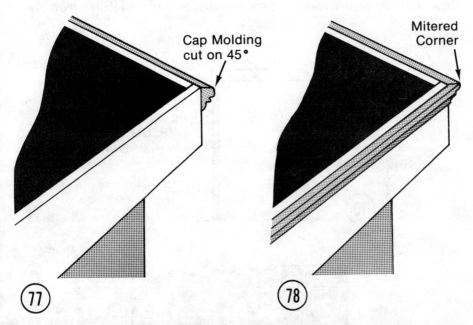

Cap Molding cut on 45°

Mitered Corner

(77)   (78)

Those who want to install a skylight should frame opening and make the installation. Complete directions begin on page 95. Those who don't need a skylight should apply roofing.

Measure dormer roof and buy shingles that match those on roof. Apply according to manufacturer's directions. Embed all shingles adjacent to step flashing in asphalt cement. If you find it necessary to renail any shingles, cover nailheads with cement.

Use matching shingles to cover ridge. Cut shingles to size of existing ridge shingles.

WINDOW INSTALLATION

Buy windows complete with exterior and interior trim. Tell retailer what thickness wall paneling or gypsum board you plan on using inside, also thickness of exterior sheathing, Illus. 79. He can then furnish windows with casings that fit.

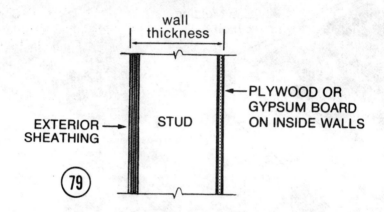

wall thickness

PLYWOOD OR GYPSUM BOARD ON INSIDE WALLS

STUD

EXTERIOR SHEATHING

79

80

Follow window manufacturer's directions. Prime coat wood windows if same wasn't done at factory. Place windows in opening. Shim in level position using pieces of shingle. When plumb and level, nail in place using 10 penny finishing nails, Illus. 80.

Before nailing permanently, test open window to make certain it works freely. If window moves freely, use a nailset to countersink nails. This prevents marring casing. Fill holes with putty.

Nail flashing window manufacturer provides in position shown, Illus. 81.

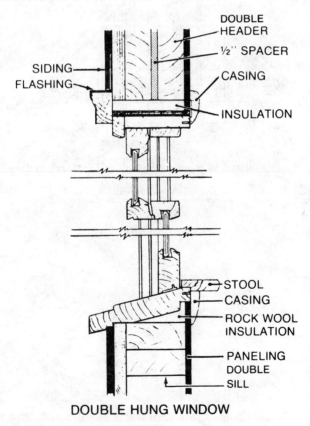

DOUBLE HUNG WINDOW

FRAMING FOR AIR CONDITIONER

If you want to install an air conditioning unit, frame opening with double 2 x 4 header and sill, Illus. 82, 95. Cut opening along inside edge of stud. Nail exterior siding to header and sill. Install conditioner following manufacturer's directions. Be sure to calk opening where manufacturer specifies.

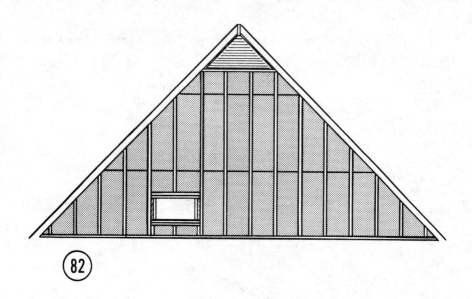

82

LOUVER INSTALLATION

If there are no louvers presently venting your attic, install one at each end, Illus. 83, above ceiling joists. Install metal louver shown or use louvers stamped out of siding. Draw location and drill ¾ or 1" holes to receive a keyhole or saber saw. Saw opening. Frame opening, Illus. 84. Nail header to studs with 16 penny nails in position shown. Screw louver in position to framing. The size of louver is important and is determined by the amount of space to be ventilated. Your retailer can estimate size required.

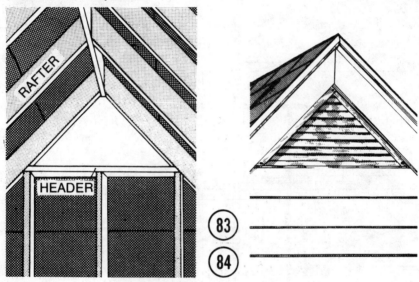

SIDING

Apply shingles or clapboard that matches siding on house. Prime coat clapboard if same wasn't primed at factory. Snap a level chalk line for first course. Estimate number of courses required to have a course level with top of window casing. Butt siding against window casings. After completing siding, calk joints where siding butts against window and door casings. Wood clapboard normally overlaps lower course ½". Courses can overlap ¾ or 1" if necessary to finish level with top of window or door frame. Drive a siding nail into each stud. Use size retailer recommends for siding purchased.

BUILD PARTITIONS

Those who plan on installing an extra bathroom or kitchen should locate same where it's convenient to existing supply and waste lines in floor below. These are usually found in one wall, Illus. 85. Ask your plumber to suggest location. By connecting to existing lines, considerable savings can be effected. Read Books #682 How to Install a Bathroom, #675 Plumbing Repairs Simplified and #608 How to Modernize a Kitchen. Each provides considerable information that turns amateurs into pros.

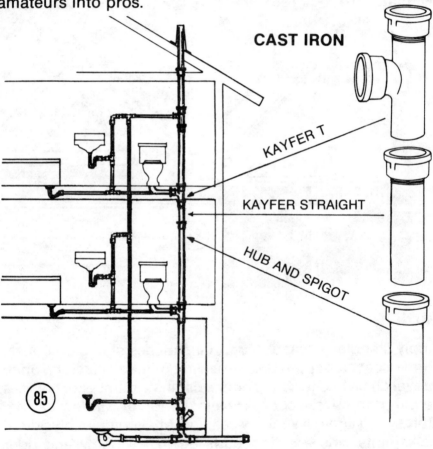

CAST IRON

KAYFER T

KAYFER STRAIGHT

HUB AND SPIGOT

85

After plumber roughs in waste, vent and supply lines, you can permanently nail subflooring in attic. When plumber specifies where he will run lines, build partitions.

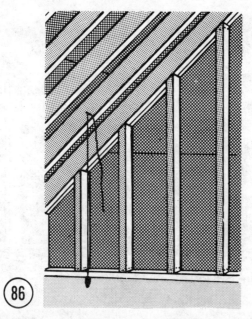

All space 4'0'' and less under rafters should be partitioned off for storage, Illus. 86.

Measure 4' on a plumb bob line. Mark four foot height on end rafters and on floor. Snap a chalk line across rafters and floor, Illus. 87. Position room edge of shoe on line, Illus, 87a. Drive 16 penny nails through shoe into joists.

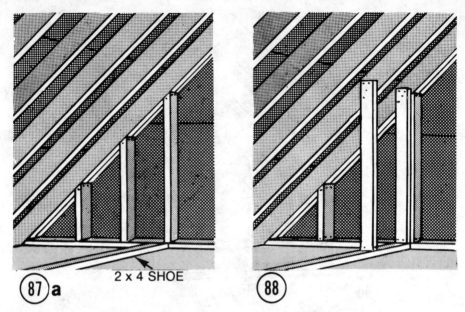

2 x 4 SHOE

⟨87⟩a ⟨88⟩

Cut 2 x 4 studs to length required. Use a level to plumb each, Illus. 88. Spike to rafters with 16 penny nails.

CAUTION: Allow space local codes specify between all framing and a chimney. This runs from 2 to 4''. Nail 2 x 4 cats, Illus. 89, to stiffen joists over dormer when framing around a chimney.

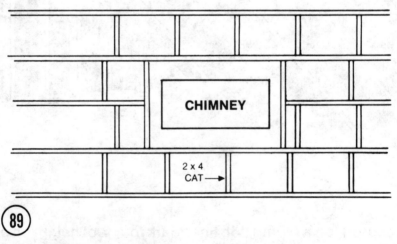

CHIMNEY

2 x 4 CAT →

⟨89⟩

Non-load bearing studs, Illus. 90, used to frame in storage partitions, can be spaced 16 or 32'' apart. Since you will want to use space behind partition for storage, frame door

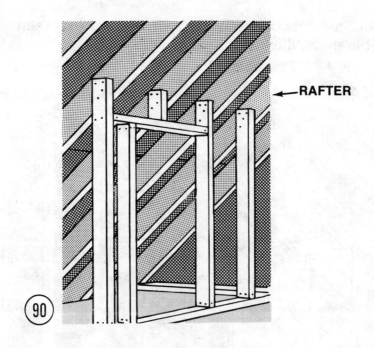

RAFTER

openings every four, six or eight feet. Nail 2 x 4 header across each opening. A plywood panel can be hinged or held in place with turn buttons, Illus. 91.

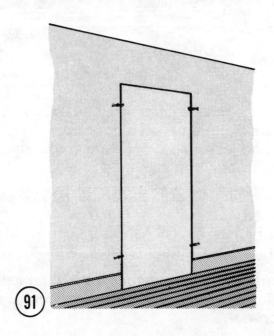

Nail 2 x 4 cats between studs, rafters, also between studs on gable ends, Illus. 92.

(92)

Build partitions to meet your needs. Use 2 x 4 for shoe, plate and studs, Illus. 93. Frame each door opening with double 2 x 4 header and jack studs. Cut shoe across door opening after nailing partition in place.

If headroom permits, a partition can be assembled on floor, raised, plumbed and nailed in place. Always nail through shoe into floor joists, except across a door opening. Where partition butts against rafters, toenail rafter to plate.

When two partitions butt together, toenail an extra stud in position indicated, Illus. 94. This provides a nailor for paneling at corner.

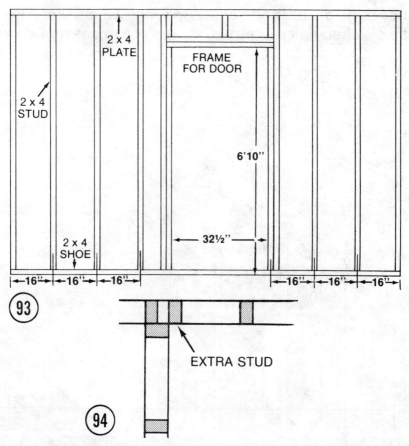

2 x 4
PLATE

2 x 4
STUD

FRAME
FOR DOOR

6'10"

2 x 4
SHOE

32½"

|←16"→|←16"→|←16"→| |←16"→|←16"→|←16"→|

(93)

EXTRA STUD

(94)

When a partition is placed between studs in a gable end, nail pieces of 2 x 4 flatwise between studs, then a 1 x 6 in position shown, Illus. 95. Position 2 x 4 blocking so the 1 x 6 finishes flush with edge of studs.

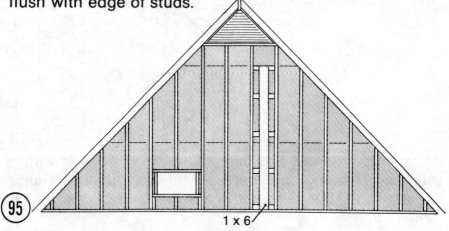

(95)

1 x 6

Since edge of studs on gable ends, Illus. 96, project beyond face of rafter, nail pieces of 2 x 4 or 2 x 6 in position shown, then a 2 x 4 or 2 x 6, Illus. 97. This provides a nailor when installing ceiling panels.

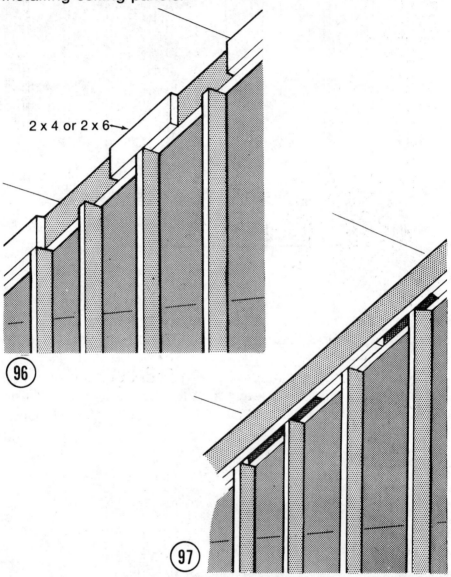

2 x 4 or 2 x 6

96

97

After all partitioning has been completed, rough in wiring, plumbing, heating, telephone, TV, air conditioning, stereo, floodlighting, burglary and/or fire alarm, etc., then install insulation.

INSULATION

After all service lines have been roughed in, apply insulation. Staple to side of studs, ceiling joists or rafters. Keep foil side of aluminum facing room.

Rock wool blankets come in 16 and 24" widths. Three different thicknesses are available. Buy 16" width for studs and rafters spaced 16" on centers; 24" width for studs and rafters 24" on centers. Buy thickness local conditions warrant. By stapling flaps to sides of studs, prefinished panels can still be applied to edge of stud with panel adhesive.

The aluminum or asphalt impregnated covering on insulation is a vapor barrier. Always keep vapor barrier facing the living, or heated area. When laying insulation in an attic over heated area below, keep vapor barrier side down. If floor joists in an attic are spaced 18" on centers, or dimension other than 16 or 24", pour loose rock wool insulation between joists. Nail plywood subflooring, Illus. 98.

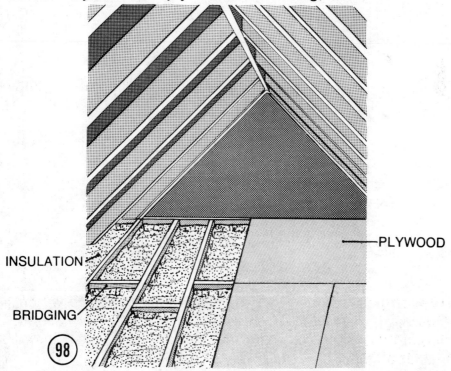

PLYWOOD

INSULATION

BRIDGING

98

Install insulation between ceiling joists before applying ceiling. Staple to ceiling joists every 8'', then continue down between rafters.

Louvers, installed at both ends of a gable roof, provide a free circulation of air above insulated area.

Insulation can be stapled every 12'' to studs on gable ends, Illus. 99.

APPLICATION OF WALLBOARD
TO CEILINGS, WALLS

Building codes frequently specify application of fire resistant asbestos or gypsum board panels. Check local codes and apply thickness specified. This must be nailed to joists every 7 to 14''. Follow manufacturer's directions.

Gypsum board panels are available in ⅜, ½ and ⅝'' thickness, in 4 x 8, 4 x 10, and up to 16' in length. Two men of comparable height, working off a raised platform, i.e., planks across the bottom step of two step ladders or from planks laid across concrete blocks, can easily handle a 4 x 8 panel. In addition to a comfortable height platform, two carpeted T's take the pressure off the installation, Illus.100.

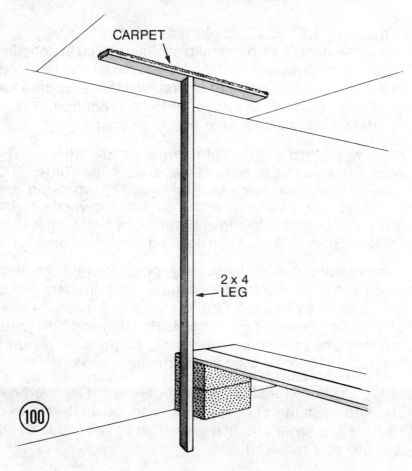

CARPET

2 x 4
LEG

100

Nail a 2 x 4 x 3'0" to a 2 x 4 leg cut to length required. Cut bottom of leg to a slight angle, Illus. 101. Staple a piece of carpet to T. After placing panel in position, kick the leg of the T in place so it holds panel snugly against joists, Illus. 100. Since the body stance and physical effort required to position and hold a panel may be difficult for those making their first installation, play safe, encourage a third person to position and kick the two T supports in place.

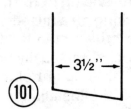

Use the largest size panels you can physically and conveniently handle with the help available. Plan installation with the fewest possible joints. All joints must be over a joist. Snap a chalk line down center of first joist that accepts a full width or length panel, or cut panel to size required. Always butt panels, edge or end, over center of joist.

Gypsum wallboard comes with various edge finishes. The tapered edge butting against tapered edge, Illus. 102, provides a finishing detail that takes joint compound and tape. Always use a hammer with a slightly crowned head. It not only drives nail into the wallboard, but also makes an indentation, Illus. 103, that can be filled with joint compound.

Due to variations that frequently occur during framing, measure space for each panel over several different areas. Cut panel to size when required to butt over center of a joist. Since a ceiling molding covers outside edge and butt joints are covered by compound and tape, beginners can do a professional job when they invest needed time.

Carefully measure location of any opening for an overhead fixture. Draw outline of opening in exact position required. Drill a hole in corner and use a keyhole or saber saw to cut opening to size required.

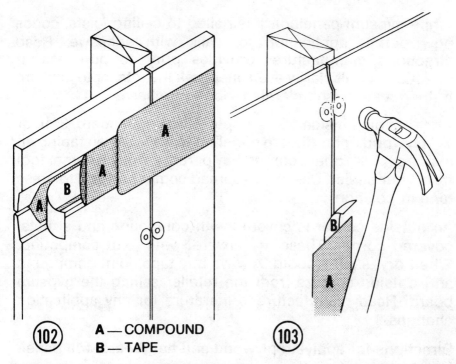

(102) A — COMPOUND
B — TAPE
(103)

Use care and a straight edge when laying out cutting lines. Draw lines on exposed face of panel. Use a straight edge and a trimming knife. Make a couple of passes at sufficient depth to permit bending scored part down. Bend to right angle. Cut through paper on bottom face. Sandpaper or file edge smooth.

Use rustproof drywall nails 1¼ to 1⅝" in length. Use size retailer recommends for thickness panel you purchase.

Taping joints is no big deal. You need a 4 to 6" putty knife to spread and force joint compound into joint. Spread compound 2" or more on both sides of joint. Smooth compound over, then apply 2" wide perforated tape. Using the wide putty knife, embed tape in compound. Do this with care so tape is completely bonded. Cover tape with joint compound. Spread it smooth over a wider surface. Feather the edges. Allow to dry overnight. Apply a second coat. This can be spread and feathered to a slightly wider area. When dry, apply a third coat over a slightly wider area. Allow this to dry, then sand surface.

While gypsum panelboard is nailed to ceiling joists, codes now permit application to walls with adhesive. Read directions manufacturer provides prior to purchase. If directions don't clarify every step, ask the retailer to explain. If the question isn't clarified, don't purchase.

After building inside stairs, apply ½" gypsum board, 3/16 or ¼" plywood or hardboard paneling to walls. When taping an inside gypsum board corner, buy or rent an inside corner tool from your dealer. Use this to spread compound and to press tape in position.

An outside corner is covered with compound and a metal covered corner. These are covered with joint compound. When dry, sand smooth. Always buy tape, joint compound and outside corners from the retailer selling the gypsum board. Read manufacturer's literature for any application changes.

Directions for applying plywood and hardboard wall paneling start on page 82.

HOW TO BUILD INSIDE STAIRS

If yours is a one story house with a ceiling opening, or access to space above ceiling joists is achieved with pulldown stairs, start reading here.

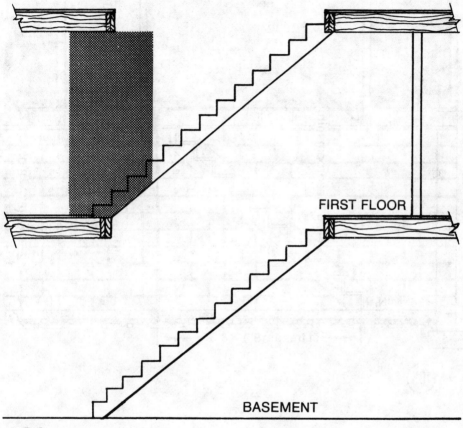

FIRST FLOOR

BASEMENT

(104)

In thousands of houses, builders placed closets on the first floor (shaded area), Illus. 104, over stairs leading to basement. In many houses the closet floor was raised, or the lower part of a back wall was sloped, Illus. 105, to provide additional headroom for basement stairs. This closet offers a prime location for stairway to "second floor." While you lose a closet, you gain a floor above. Be sure to maintain a 6'6" minimum headroom or minimum height local codes specify over basement stairs.

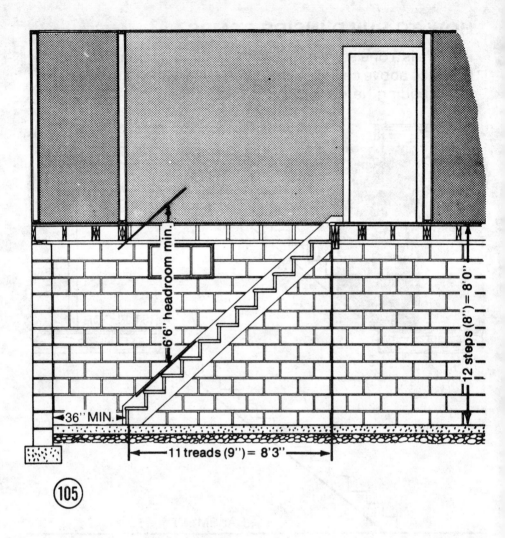

6'6" headroom min.

12 steps (8") = 8'0"

36" MIN.

11 treads (9") = 8'3"

(105)

If you don't have a closet, the space directly over basement stairs is still a choice location. If you don't have a basement, locate stairs where they are convenient to the front door.

Ascertain direction of floor joists in attic. Stair stringers can be installed parallel to joists, Illus. 106, 107, or at right angle, Illus. 108.

After selecting the location, estimate number of steps required to reach attic, also width of space required. Stock stairs run from 30 to 48" in width.

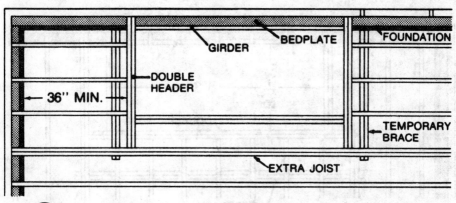

GIRDER BEDPLATE FOUNDATION

DOUBLE HEADER

36" MIN.

TEMPORARY BRACE

EXTRA JOIST

(106)

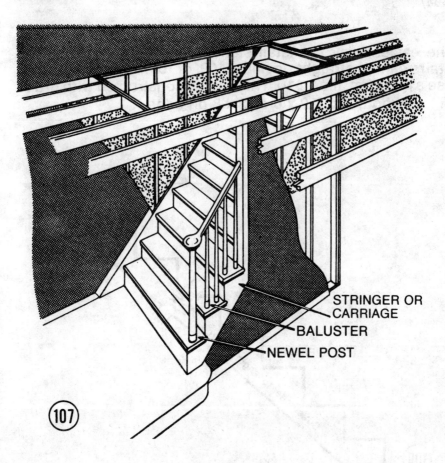

STRINGER OR CARRIAGE

BALUSTER

NEWEL POST

(107)

71

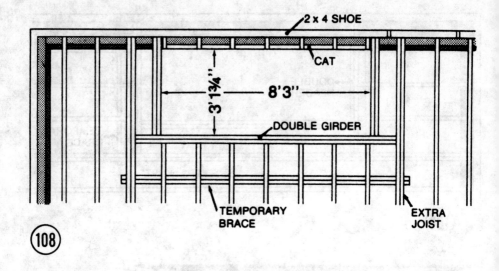

(108)

The easiest way to install stairs is along an existing wall. Stairs can go straight up, Illus. 109, or for a shorter carriage, use a platform, Illus. 110. This can be constructed with 5/8 or ¾" plywood, 2 x 4, 2 x 6 or 2 x 8 on edge.

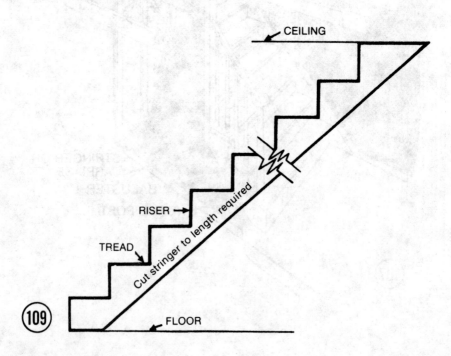

(109)

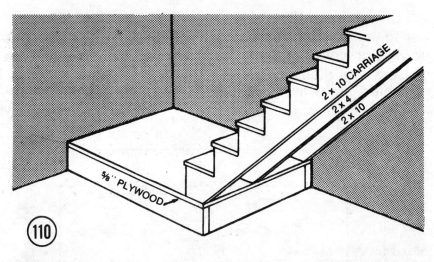

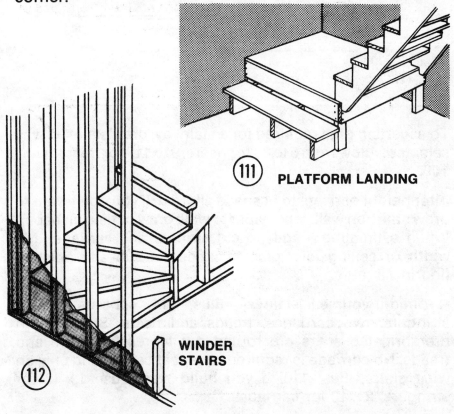

A two step platform, Illus. 111, requires an even shorter carriage. Winder stairs, Illus. 112, provide still another alternative. A platform or winder stairs can be installed in a corner.

PLATFORM LANDING

WINDER STAIRS

73

First draw a plan, Illus. 113, to indicate location. Measure floor to ceiling height, also width of joists in attic. With this information your building material dealer can estimate size and cost of a stairway. He can quote on a ready to install assembled stairway, precut parts or materials needed to build.

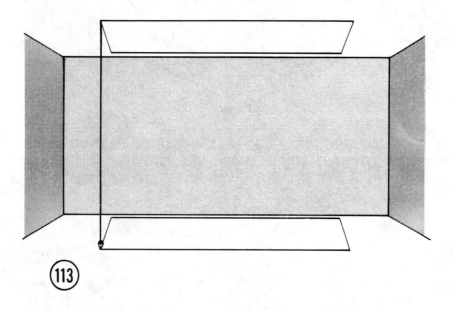

(113)

To ascertain area required for a stairway, draw stairs on wall selected. Allow from 6 to 8" for risers, 9 to 11" for treads, Illus. 109.

Alter height of risers to fit space allotted. If you don't want to draw stairs on wall, tape paper to wall, draw outline on paper. When estimating length to cut stringer and carriage, add width of ceiling joist plus thickness of sub and finished flooring in attic.

A build-it-yourself stairway, Illus. 114, consists of two stringers, two carriages, treads and risers. Stringers on prefabricated stairs are routed out to receive risers and treads. No carriage is required except at center, and only on wide stairs, Illus. 110. If you build stairs, use 1 x 12 for stringers, 2 x 10 for carriages.

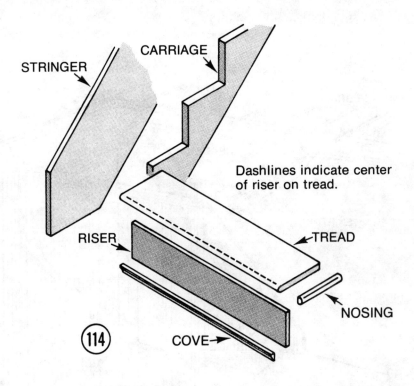

STRINGER

CARRIAGE

Dashlines indicate center
of riser on tread.

RISER

TREAD

NOSING

(114)

COVE

Ask your dealer to check the job to insure getting accurate measurements. Make certain location of existing doors permits installing an assembled stairway. Don't order a stairway based on your measurements.

If you cut and frame opening in ceiling to size dealer specifies for stairs ordered, two men can raise and nail same in place on delivery.

If distance from a stair builder increases the cost of an assembled stairway, buy precut parts, assemble them yourself. This can be done on the floor. The assembled stairway can then be raised and nailed in position, or you can assemble in position.

Those purchasing precut parts can buy stringers routed out for treads and risers. If this is unavailable, nail precut carriage, Illus. 115, to stringer, Illus. 116.

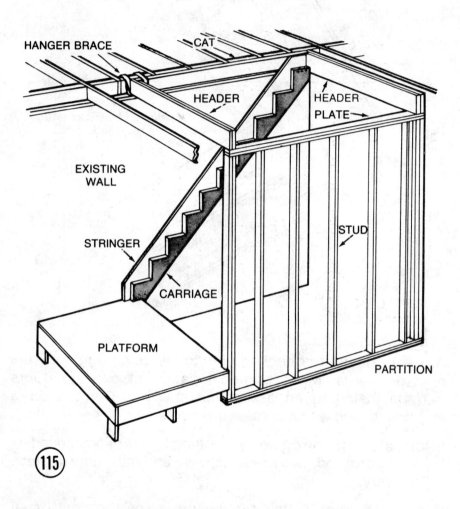

HANGER BRACE

CAT

HEADER

HEADER
PLATE

EXISTING
WALL

STRINGER

STUD

CARRIAGE

PLATFORM

PARTITION

(115)

While two carriages will support most stairs, use three for 48''
or wider installation. Risers are nailed to carriage with 8
penny finishing nails. The treads are then nailed in place.

Next nail riser to tread, Illus. 117.

Follow stair builder's directions when assembling precut
parts. Countersink all nail heads. Fill holes with wood filler.

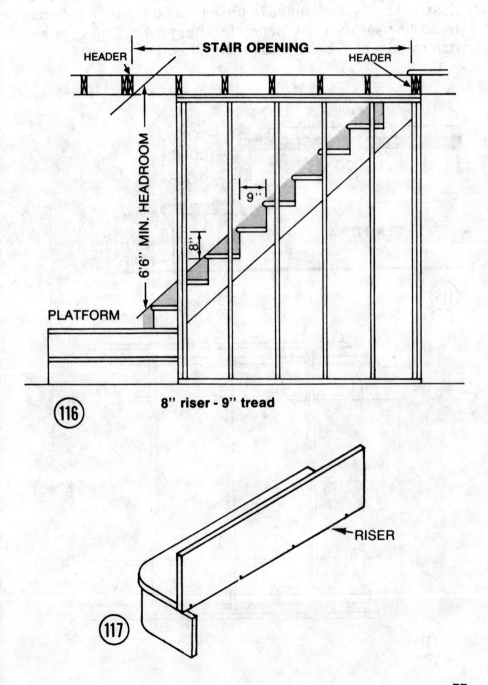

STAIR OPENING

HEADER

HEADER

6'6" MIN. HEADROOM

9"

8"

PLATFORM

(116)

8" riser - 9" tread

RISER

(117)

NOTE: Apply glue to carriage before installing a riser or tread. Apply glue to back edge of tread before installing. Using a square, locate and draw a line to indicate center of riser, Illus. 114. Drill holes to prevent splitting, then face nail tread to riser using 10 penny finishing nails. Drill riser and nail tread with 6 penny box nails, Illus. 118.

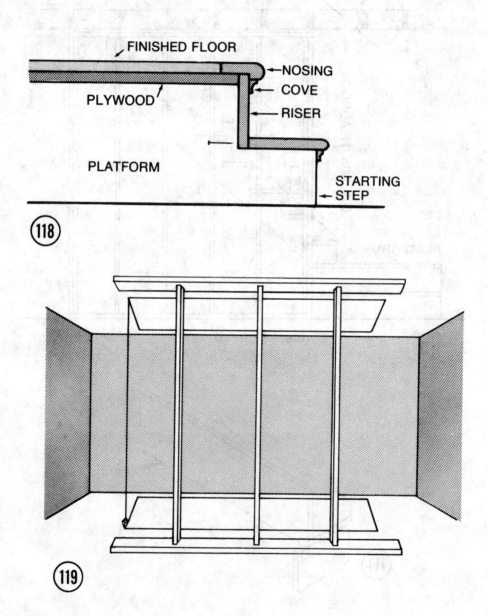

Apply glue to wedges supplied by stair builder. Drive in position under treads and risers to lock both in position.

When you know how many steps are required, you can then draw lines to indicate opening for stairs on ceiling. Drop a plumb bob down from each corner of proposed opening to accurately draw outline on floor, Illus. 113.

Before cutting, brace joists with 2 x 6 plate, shoe and 2 x 4 studs, Illus. 119. Allow space so you can erect a partition, Illus. 115.

If you locate stairs away from an existing wall, brace on both sides and build two partitions.

To facilitate working on ceiling, place planks across two step ladders at a height that permits sawing through ceiling.

A saber saw simplifies cutting opening in plaster. Proceed cautiously so you don't drill or saw through BX or any water line that may cross opening. If BX crosses opening selected, pull fuse and relocate line with a junction box and an extra length of BX cable. Consult Book #694 Electrical Repairs Simplified for complete details.

If you don't have power tools, drill a ½ or ¾" hole in each corner of drawn outline. Use a keyhole or compass saw, then a crosscut saw. Cut opening in ceiling plaster large enough to permit crawling into area.

Once top side, lay out guide lines and saw joists to size opening requires. Cut and nail headers in position, Illus. 107, 108. Use lumber same size as floor joists. Nail joists to header.

Install a double girder and header around opening. Use steel hanger brackets, Illus. 115, to reinforce headers.

If building stairs against an existing wall, remove shoe molding, baseboard and ceiling molding on wall selected.

Locate studs and nail through stringer into each stud and header. Stringer finishes flush with finished flooring in attic.

A starting platform can be one or two steps high, Illus. 110, 111. Build to width of stairs and to length desired. Cut 2 x 4 legs to height platform requires. Notch studs if you use 2 x 8 for frame.

Illus. 116 shows how a partition can be framed into a platform.

Nail ⅝" plywood to floor of platform.

Use a starting step, Illus. 117, available from your lumber dealer. Nail riser to starting step. Nail through riser into platform. Platform can be covered with finished flooring and nosing, Illus. 118. Use 1 x 6 or 1 x 8 as a temporary step if you want to save finished treads until after attic modernization is completed.

Your lumber dealer supplies stock stair nosing, cove, along with rails, balustrades, etc.

Fasten stair railing in position following dealer's directions. Space beneath stairs provide excellent storage area, Illus. 120, 121.

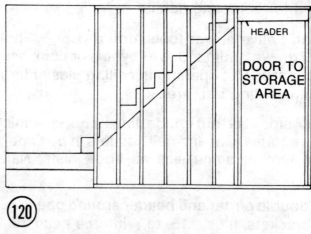

HEADER

DOOR TO STORAGE AREA

(120)

If you plan on using 4 x 8 or 4 x 10' plywood or gypsum board panels in attic, estimate number required and pass these up through opening before installing stairs. An easy way to handle these panels with a minimum of help is shown in Illus. 122. Build a 2 x 4 x 10' or height easel required.

80

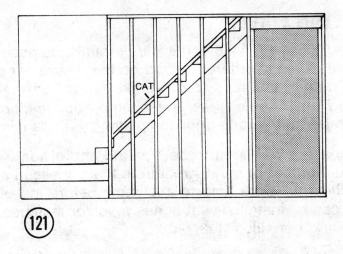

(121)

Use 2 x 4 x 10' for A, 2 x 4 x 3' for B, 2 x 8 for C, 1 x 4 for D. Spike B to A, C to B, A to C, D to edge of C. Load panels on easel. If you work alone, use a length of clothes line with an 8' plus loop. Slip loop over a panel. Pull with rope. The same easel, built to height required, can be used to hoist panels into attic after you cut opening for a dormer.

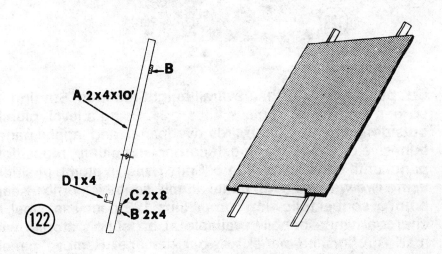

(122)

81

PANELING WALLS

3/16 and ¼" 4 x 7, 4 x 8 and 4 x 10' prefinished paneling is available in many different wood grains. These handsome panels permit amateurs to make like "pros" on their first paneling job. In some areas, codes require application of ½" gypsum board to studs prior to covering with paneling.

Next measure wall area to be covered and divide by 4' to estimate number of panels required. Place these in attic at the earliest possible time to acclimate before installation. Panels can be installed with adhesive, color matched nails, or a nailing gun, Illus. 123.

(123)

Cut panels ½" less than overall height required. Starting in corner, butt panel in place, Illus. 124. Using a level, plumb outside edge. If plumb, remove panel and apply panel adhesive or nail to framing. If corner isn't plumb, reposition panel until edge reads plumb. Shim panel in plumb position using two wedges. With panel plumb, scribe to corner. Keep point of scriber following corner, Illus. 125, pencil on panel. A charcoal white pencil (available at art supply stores) will mark prefinished panel without damage. Remove panel.

Saw, file or plane edge to scribed line. Replace panel. Check with level. When plumb, remove panel and apply adhesive. Again reset panel with two nails about 16" in along top edges. Press panel in place, then pull out and block bottom end from wall following adhesive manufacturer's directions. Allow adhesive to set 6 to 8 minutes or time specified before pressing panel back into position. Pound panel in place using a carpet or towel covered piece of 2 x 4 and a hammer.

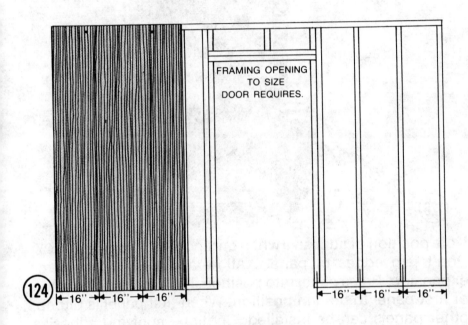

FRAMING OPENING
TO SIZE
DOOR REQUIRES.

124 ⊢16"⊣⊢16"⊣⊢16"⊣ ⊢16"⊣⊢16"⊣⊢16"⊣

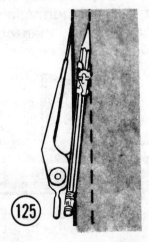

125

Panel adhesive simplifies installation, but it should only be applied in temperatures ranging from 60 to 90°. When panels are fastened directly to studs, apply a 3" ribbon of ⅛" thick adhesive every 6", to all intermediate studs. Use a calking gun, Illus. 126. Apply a continuous ⅛" bead along shoe, plate, cats, headers and those studs behind edge of panel.

(126)

Note position of adhesive when butting two panels, Illus. 127. Don't jam edges of panels. Allow about ⅛" spacing for expansion. Press panel into position. Drive two nails into top of first panel to hold in position. When first panel is plumb, other panels can be installed. Continue applying adhesive and pressing each panel in position. Allow each to set time adhesive manufacturer specifies, then pound panel along framing. Use a padded 2 x 4.

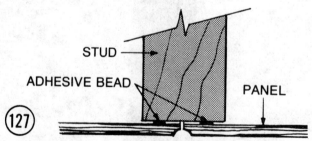

STUD

ADHESIVE BEAD

PANEL

(127)

Paint exposed face of stud black or use black tape. Apply adhesive to stud, not to tape.

An adhesive cartridge permits installation of four to six 4 x 8' panels. Since manufacturers frequently change formulas, always read and follow directions manufacturer specifies.

One trick of the trade suggests using black tape on studs or over wallboard at each joint, Illus. 127.

If panels are to be nailed, do so every 6" along outer edges, every 12" to intermediate studs. A nailing gun, Illus. 123, speeds installation. If grooved paneling is being installed, nail panel as shown, Illus. 128. Avoid nailing in grooves. Always match groove over a stud.

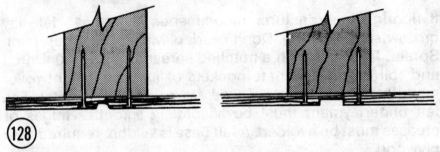

Walls that require more than a 7 or 8' panel can be handled as shown in Illus. 129. The panel is nailed snug to ceiling. Scrap lengths of ¼" plywood, cut to width required, are used as spacers. A 6 or 8" base, cut from matching prefinished paneling, to length needed, is nailed in place. Always match grain with panel on wall. In this installation, use shoe molding.

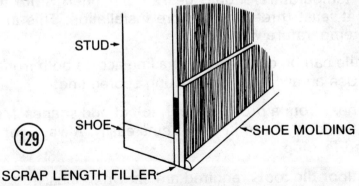

STUD

SHOE

SHOE MOLDING

SCRAP LENGTH FILLER

Book #605, How to Apply Paneling, provides considerably more detailed information on this subject.

HOW TO LAY FLOOR TILE

These directions simplify laying 9 x 9" asphalt and vinyl tiles over plywood or hardboard. Since there are many manufacturers, and each offers an adhesive, buy adhesive when you buy tiles. Follow their directions.

Adhesive permits laying tile directly to plywood, hardboard or particle board. In every case the surface must be smooth, level, all cracks filled and sanded smooth. The surface must be free of dust, paint, wax, other finishes, etc. Use a damp cloth to pick up dust if you sand floor.

If flooring manufacturer recommends laying #15 felt, lay crosswise to flooring. Don't overlap. Make a neat butt joint. Spread felt paste with a notched spreader, Illus. 130. Unroll and roll felt to eliminate pockets of air. Use weight roller manufacturer suggests. These are available on rental. The felt underlayment must be absolutely smooth. Ridges or creases must be avoided. A felt base is seldom required over plywood.

Asphalt tile comes in 9 x 9" size, 1/8 and 3/16" thick. 12 x 12" is available on special order. 1/8" thickness is the most popular. These are packed 80 pieces to a carton; 54 pieces to a carton 3/16" thick.

Do not attempt to lay tiles in a cold room or on a cold floor. Room temperature should be 72° or higher. Store tile in room at least three days before installation. This insures room temperature when laid.

Floor tile can be cut by scoring a line across both front and back. Use an awl, then snap along scored line.

Apply heat from a propane torch to cut odd shapes. Merely warm tile, don't burn it, and it cuts easily. Always cut with finished face up.

Other floor tile tools required are shown in Illus. 130.

First locate exact center of room. Measure distance A and B, Illus. 131.

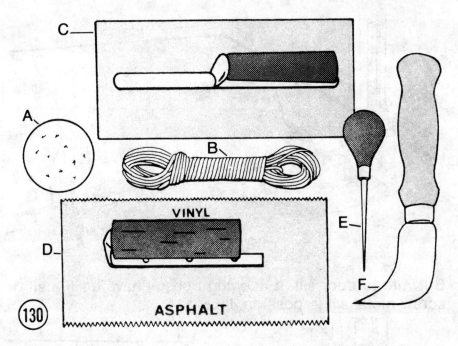

(130)

A — CHALK
B — CHALK LINE
C — MASON'S TROWEL

D — NOTCHED SPREADER
E — AWL
F — LINOLEUM KNIFE

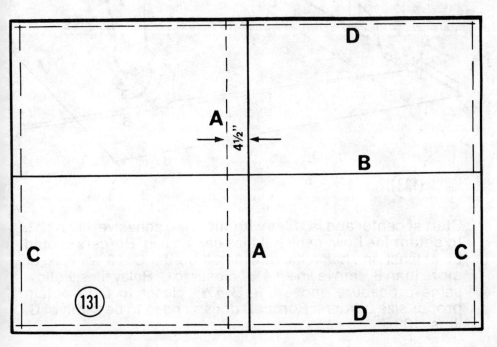

(131)

4½"

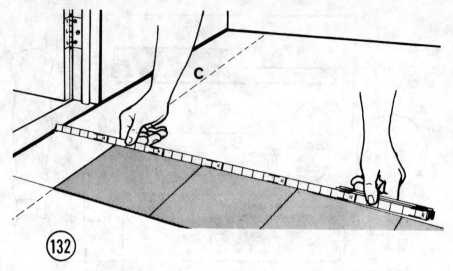

(132)

Butt tile to door sill. If opening doesn't have a sill, nail or screw metal sill in position, Illus. 134.

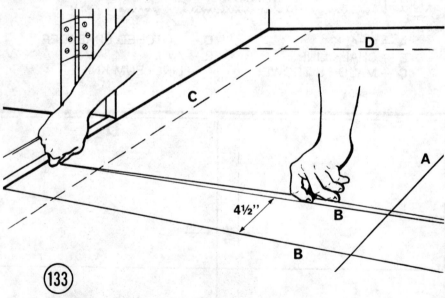

(133)

Start at center and lay tiles without using adhesive, Illus. 132, to determine how many full tiles can be laid. Borders should be at least one half a tile or wider. If border C is 2" or less, or more than 8", move line A 4½" closer to C. Relay tiles. Follow same procedure, move line B 4½" closer to D to obtain proper size borders. Border D doesn't need to be width of C, Illus. 133.

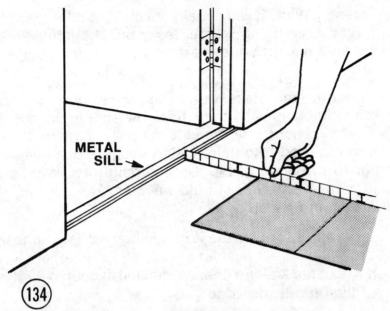

METAL
SILL →

(134)

Start at center point and spread adhesive following manufacturer's directions, Illus. 135. Do one quarter of a room at a time. Use a notched trowel, Illus. 130. Holding at about a 45° angle, use a sweeping motion. If you go over a chalk line, allow adhesive to set, then snap a new chalk line.

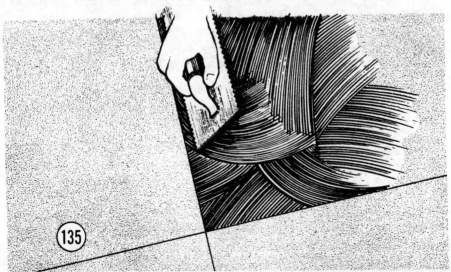

(135)

Spread adhesive evenly. Follow manufacturer's directions explicitly. Don't leave any globs. If you do, it will work up between tiles. Allow adhesive to set time manufacturer recommends. While it will usually set up in 15 minutes to half hour, don't rush. It should feel tacky but shouldn't stick to your finger. Since the adhesive remains alive for days, there's no rush.

Start at center and place, don't slide tile in position. Make certain tile lines up with chalk line. Tile should be laid with ends flush and tight. Lay each tile in position with pattern in direction required to obtain design desired. Use head of a hammer to rub edge of tile for a smooth joint. Wipe away excess adhesive, if you should have any, as you go. Use cleaner recommended by tile manufacturer.

To fit a border tile, place tile X in position without adhesive, Illus. 136. Place tile Y against a wall, sill, cabinet, etc. Draw line on X. Cut tile X along line. Lay full tile in course for X and use cut tile on outside edge.

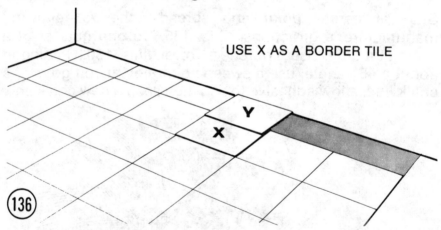

USE X AS A BORDER TILE

Follow same procedure to fit each piece of border tile. Since tile Y will get dirty, use it over and over. Left over pieces of border tile can be cut to size required to cover kickboard on base cabinet.

Roll each quarter of floor with a roller before starting next quarter. If you have to make odd shaped cutouts for pipes, first make a paper pattern. When it's right, trace it on tile. Heat tile, then cut to shape required. Tin snips frequently simplify cutting certain shapes. Household scissors can be used to cut vinyl.

In most cases you can pry up a radiator or range to slip tile under or cut tile to fit. Use a piece of 2 x 4 and a prybar. In this case it will be necessary to apply adhesive to tile. Most gas and electric ranges can be raised sufficiently to permit inserting tile.

NOTE: Matching base is readily available. This permits covering joint between last tile and base cabinet. Use adhesive manufacturer recommends when installing base, Illus. 137.

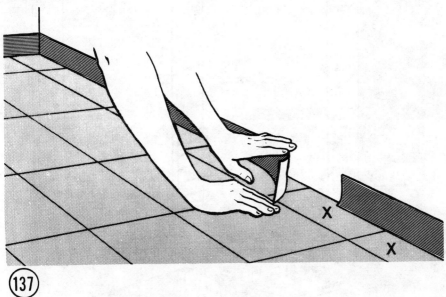

(137)

Manufacturers sell colorful tile inserts and strips that can be worked into a floor. These add a note of distinction and are well worth installing.

Large size border tiles are also available. These simplify fitting a border tile to door casing, sill, etc. Scribe border tiles that butt against an irregularity. Always cut a border tile just a hair over size so it fits snug.

Heat edge that butts against baseboard, cabinet or other projection, over a propane torch. Press the soft edge into position. Use a piece of 1 x 2 to press softened tile smooth.

Install a metal sill across door opening if it doesn't have a wood sill, Illus. 134.

HANG DOORS

Use 3½ x 3½" loose pin butt hinges. Mortise hinge in door 6" down from top, 8½" up from bottom, third hinge at center. Place hinge in position and mark outline on edge of door. Using a 1" chisel, make cuts to depth equal to thickness of hinge leaf, Illus. 138, 139. Chisel out mortise, Illus. 140. Fasten leaf, Illus. 141. Mortise jamb following same procedure.

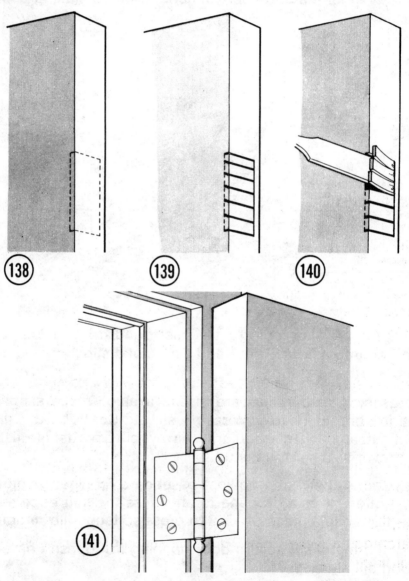

PREFINISHED WOOD MOLDINGS

Wood and vinyl covered moldings, Illus. 142, simplify trimming walls, ceiling, doors and windows. The shoe can be used with or without a base.

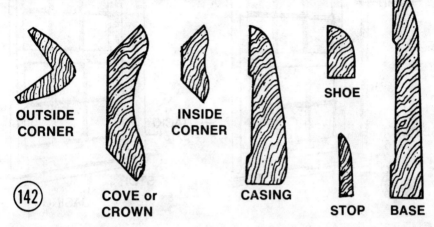

OUTSIDE CORNER

INSIDE CORNER

SHOE

142

COVE or CROWN

CASING

STOP   BASE

DESCRIPTION	SIZE	METRIC	LTH.METRIC
Shoe	⅝ x 5/16"	1.6 x .8cm	10' — 304.8cm
Stop	1 5/16 x 5/16"	3.3 x .8	10'
Casing	½ x 2¼"	1.3 x 5.7	7' — 213.4
Casing	½ x 2¼"	1.3 x 5.7	10'
Base	13/32 x 3"	1.0 x 7.6	10'
Outside Corner	⅞ x ⅞"	2.2 x 2.2	8' — 243.8
Inside Corner	¾ x ¾"	1.9 x 1.9	8'
Cove	9/16 x 2¼"	1.4 x 5.7	10'

Use the stop and casing to trim a window or door, Illus. 143. Casing can also be used as a chair rail. Use outside and inside corners where noted.

A cove is frequently used instead of a crown molding at ceiling, Illus. 144. When applying casing to windows and doors, miter cut top ends 45° and cut to length required. Apply adhesive to miter joint, then nail casing in place with 4 penny finishing nails. The miter joint can be touched up with matching putty stik. Install door casing before installing base molding.

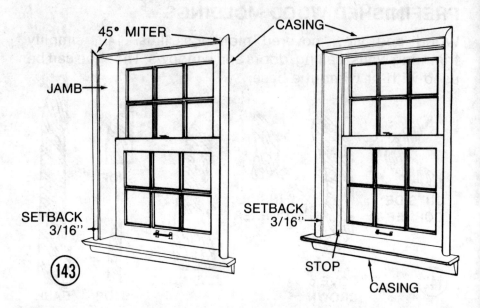

If wall to wall carpeting is to be installed, butt carpeting to panel. No base is required. Book #683, Carpeting Simplified, provides complete details for laying carpeting.

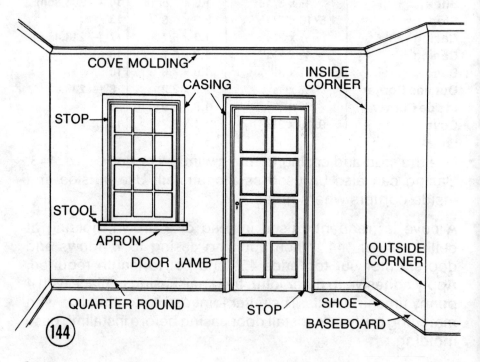

HOW TO INSTALL A SKYLIGHT

At time of publication, space used for business purpose was considered tax deductible. While you can expect the IRS to question same, many homeowners are even getting religion when they discover mail order ordained ministers get preferential tax treatment. If there's an artist, architect, designer or doctor in the family who needs or prefers daylight, consider installation of a skylight. Prefabricated skylights, Illus. 145, are relatively easy to install. Stock sizes range from 16 x 34'', 16 x 48'', 24 x 24'', 24 x 48'', 32 x 32'', 32 x 48'', 48 x 48''.

(145)

The 16 x 24'' or 16 x 48'' is one of the easiest to install since it's positioned over a pair of rafters spaced 16'' on centers. The 24'' wide skylight was designed for houses where rafters are spaced 24'' on centers. The 32'' width requires cutting one rafter; the 48'' width requires cutting two rafters. To provide directions that cover installation of all sizes, we explain installation of a 32 x 32'' skylight. This requires cutting through one rafter.

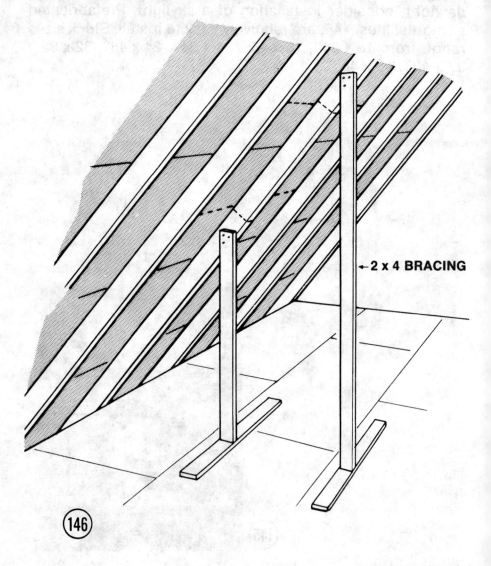

←2 x 4 BRACING

(146)

The first step is to select inside space where daylight is needed. Go outside to see if trees cast a shadow over area selected during the periods the light is needed. Draw outline of opening on inside of roof, Illus. 146.

Build a curb, Illus. 147, to fit skylight selected. Cut opening in roof to inside dimension of curb.

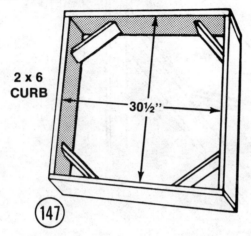

2 x 6
CURB

30½"

(147)

Brace rafters before cutting, Illus. 146. For a 32 x 32" skylight, build a 2 x 6 curb with 30½ x 30½ inside dimensions, Illus. 147. This curb will fit directly over rafters spaced 16" on centers. Check corners with square. Hold square with blocks nailed temporarily in corners.

Since a considerable amount of work can be done by working from inside attic, build a platform at sufficient height to allow you to stand halfway through roof opening. Nail 2 x 4 posts to floor and rafters. Nail 2 x 4 cross ties to posts at required height. Temporarily nail a panel of ¾" plywood to cross ties for working platform.

Due to the variance in lumber thickness, and difference in framing instructions provided by manufacturers of prefabricated skylights, dimensions we suggest must be altered to meet those specified. For a 32 x 32" skylight, cut rafter 33⅝", but do not cut into roof sheathing. Remove cut rafter. Saw sheathing and roofing 30⅜" along rafters, then between rafters, Illus. 148, 149.

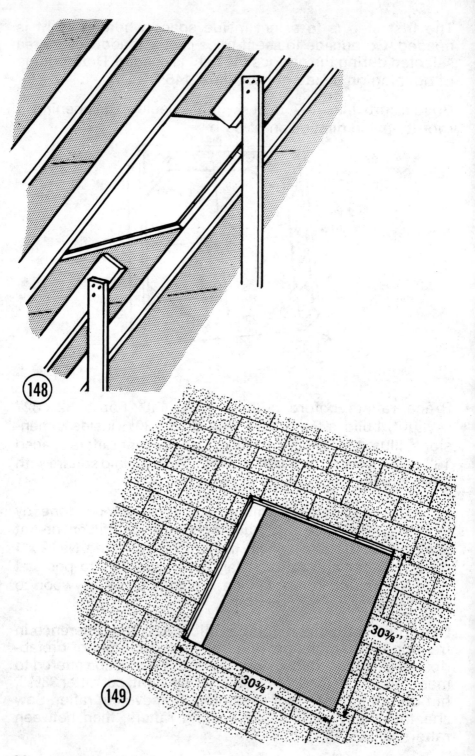

(148)

(149) 30⅜"

30⅜"

98

The opening now measures 30⅜ x 30⅜", Illus. 149. Place assembled curb around top of opening. Use chalk, draw a line around base of curb, Illus. 150.

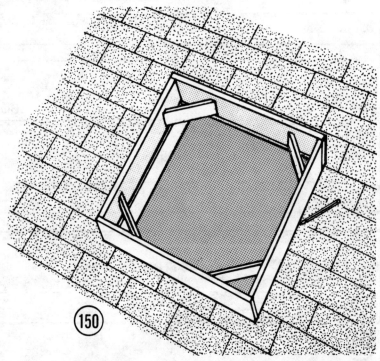

Remove curb. Cut shingles along chalk line, Illus. 151. This permits curb to butt against felt.

Using chisel end of a wrecking bar, or long chisel, loosen and remove those shingle nails within 4" of opening, Illus. 152.

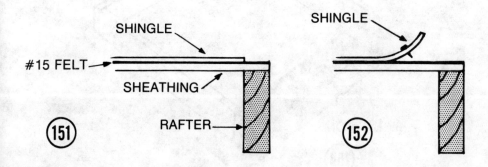

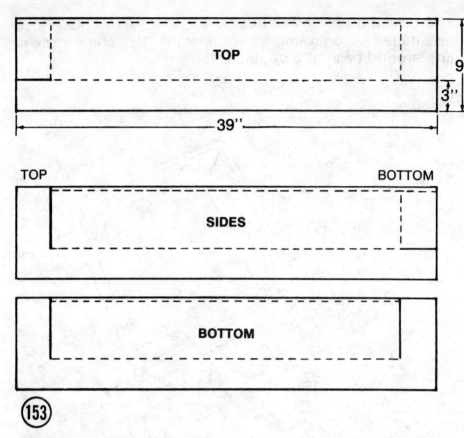

TOP

9"

3"

39"

TOP   BOTTOM

SIDES

BOTTOM

(153)

Cut and bend four strips of aluminum flashing, 9 x 39", Illus. 153. Solid lines indicate where flashing is cut; dash lines indicate where flashing is bent.

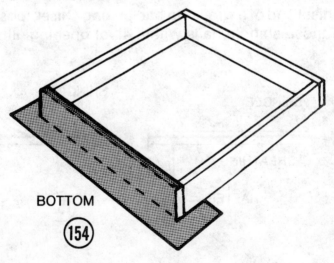

BOTTOM

(154)

Using curb as a form, bend bottom flashing to shape shown, Illus. 154.

Bend sides in position shown, Illus. 155, then bend top. Identify flashing — top, side, bottom, then remove from curb.

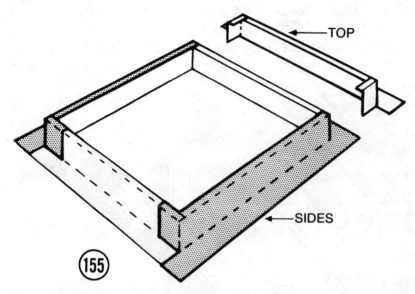

Lift loosened shingles, remove nails within 4'' of opening and apply roofing cement over felt, Illus. 152.

Apply roofing cement between flashing and shingle. Insert 3'' strip of flashing under shingle, press shingles into position, bend flashing away from opening, Illus. 156.

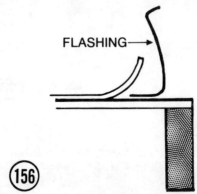

Following same procedure, slip side flashing, then top strip in position.

Nail through sheathing into curb with 16 penny common nails, Illus. 157. Toenail through inside edge of curb, into rafters, with 8 penny nails.

Bend bottom flashing into position. Nail top edge to curb, Illus. 158. Use 1'' aluminum nails with aluminum, spaced about 12'' apart. Next bend and nail side flashing, then top flashing. You can either solder corners or bond with epoxy. Do not nail. You can nail shingles up to, but not through flashing. Paint exposed shingle nailheads with roofing cement.

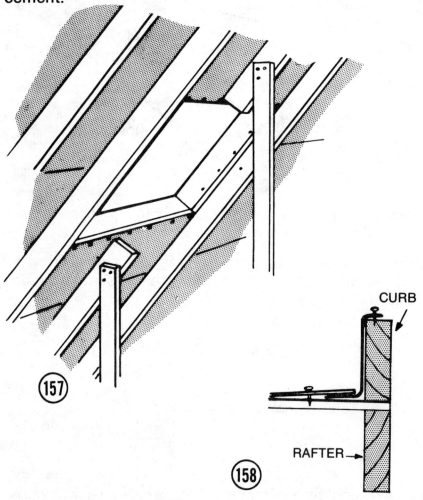

CURB

RAFTER→

(157)

(158)

Cut headers, Illus. 159, to length required. Nail rafters to header. You can now remove 2 x 4 bracing.

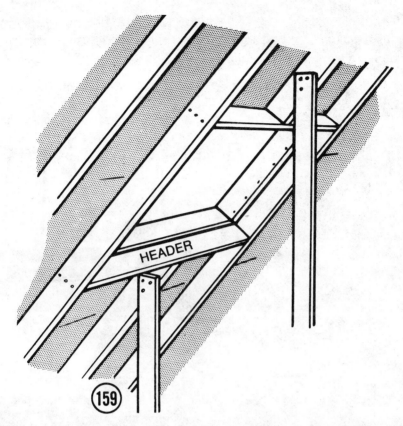

HEADER

(159)

Nailing to top of curb is optional. Most skylight frames provide a tight, waterproof seal.

The skylight can now be fastened in position. While installation of skylight shown, Illus. 160, requires no further waterproofing, if you want to run a ⅛" thick ribbon of silicone sealant around top edge of curb, it will bond aluminum frame to top of curb.

Fasten skylight to curb with 16 roundhead aluminum screws provided by manufacturer. The inside face of curb, rafter and ceiling joist can be covered with a ¼" hardboard panel, then painted with ceiling paint.

A matching ceiling panel, complete with hinge strip, can be fastened to ceiling. Skylight manufacturer provides a hinge strip that can be screwed to inside of opening. The ceiling panel slips into hinge.

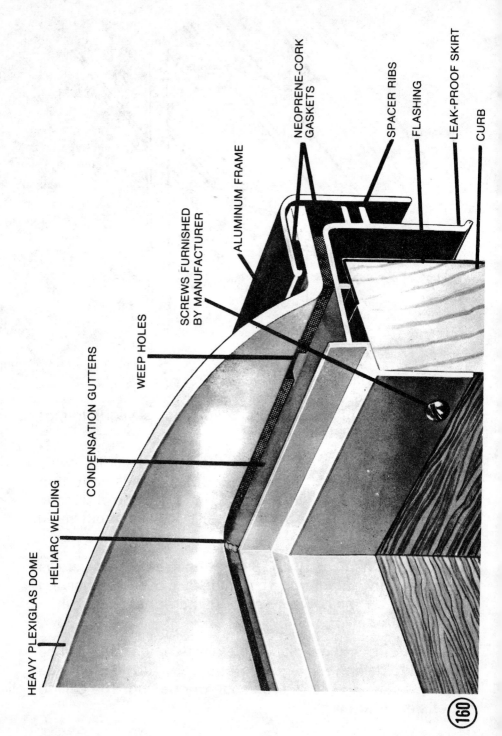

NEOPRENE-CORK GASKETS

SPACER RIBS

FLASHING

LEAK-PROOF SKIRT

CURB

ALUMINUM FRAME

SCREWS FURNISHED BY MANUFACTURER

WEEP HOLES

CONDENSATION GUTTERS

HELIARC WELDING

HEAVY PLEXIGLAS DOME

160

104

A SECOND FLOOR APARTMENT

Through the years one's lifestyle is influenced by events beyond our control. Almost before we realize the passage of time, children leave home and a once crowded house seems empty. Children grow, get married or divorced. Houses, like people, must adjust to current needs. Time also creates aging parents.

Transforming heated but unused second floor bedrooms into a completely separate apartment with outside stairs can fill an important need. It not only provides low cost, desperately needed housing, but also saves considerable energy.

The success of a conversion of this kind requires outside stairs, Illus. 2, against side of house, or to a sundeck, Illus. 161. It requires installation of a kitchen or kitchenette on the second floor, and usually a bathroom on the first floor. If you position the kitchenette against the wall containing waste and supply lines, Illus. 162, it greatly simplifies installation. If necessary, supply and waste lines can be enclosed within a sliding or bifolding door closet* on the floor below. Installing a bathroom on the first floor, below existing one, simplifies installation. Book #682 How to Install an Extra Bathroom helps save a bundle. By doing what directions suggest, a plumber can make necessary code approved connections in a minimum of time.

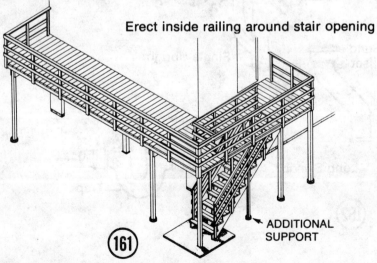

Erect inside railing around stair opening

161

ADDITIONAL
SUPPORT

*Read Book #634 How to Build Storage Units.

Typical 2 Bathroom
Cast Iron Soil Stack

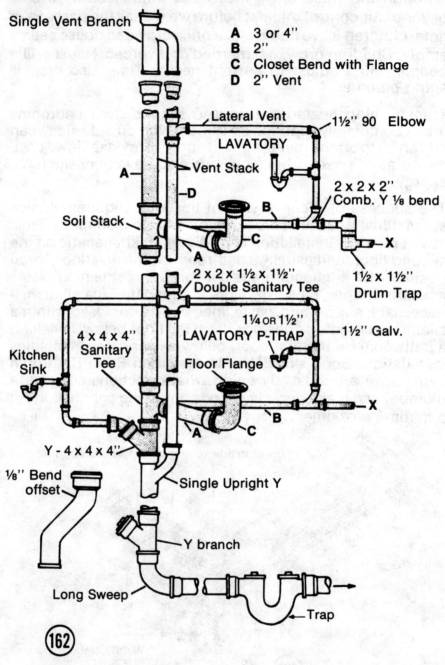

Single Vent Branch

A 3 or 4''
B 2''
C Closet Bend with Flange
D 2'' Vent

Lateral Vent

1½'' 90 Elbow

LAVATORY

Vent Stack

A

D

2 x 2 x 2''
Comb. Y ⅛ bend

Soil Stack

B

C

X

A

1½ x 1½''
Drum Trap

2 x 2 x 1½ x 1½''
Double Sanitary Tee

1¼ OR 1½''

LAVATORY P-TRAP

1½'' Galv.

4 x 4 x 4''
Sanitary
Tee

Kitchen
Sink

Floor Flange

A

B

C

X

Y - 4 x 4 x 4''

Single Upright Y

⅛'' Bend
offset

Y branch

Long Sweep

Trap

(162)

106

Before spending money for materials, take a pad of paper. Measure second floor space. Shop around and note the many strip kitchen "packages" currently available. Draw a plan, Illus. 163. Allow for living and dining space.

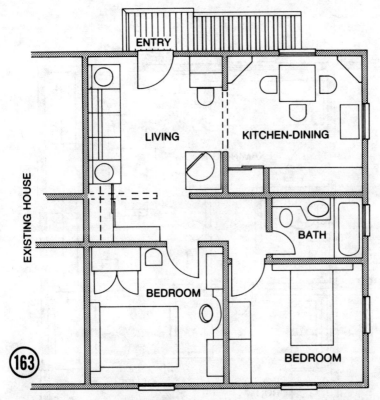

Go shopping to ascertain the cost of all equipment, air conditioning, etc., needed to convert a second floor. If you plan on using space in an attic as a second floor bedroom to a second floor apartment, add cost of stair materials. Consider the many options. If a parent needs ground level living space, will you feel comfortable living in an air conditioned second floor apartment? Does the planned use of available space provide the privacy both families need? Can the overall cost of materials be recouped in savings effected?

A factor of prime interest to zoning boards is the energy saved. Since heat rises, every furnace heats a second floor even when the thermostat is turned down. The BTU's needed for two families costs only slightly more than for one.

The creation of a second floor apartment is predicated on obtaining a permit. This will be evaluated on who is to use the space. Where hardship requires the renovation, permits are generally granted.

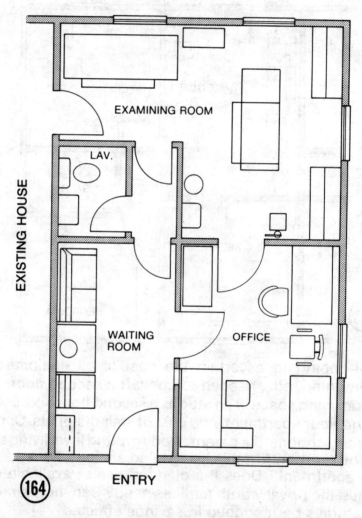

EXAMINING ROOM

LAV.

EXISTING HOUSE

WAITING ROOM

OFFICE

(164) ENTRY

If space is needed for a doctor or dentist, Illus. 164, artist, real estate or other office in the home, consider both the tax benefits plus super savings in time and gasoline. An office at home provides many more hours to enjoy your work or living, while it saves gallons of gasoline.

108

INSTALLATION OF AN OUTSIDE DOOR

The successful use of a second floor apartment requires PRIVACY. This usually necessitates installation of outside stairs and a second floor entry door. Stairs should be constructed where they are convenient to a driveway or sidewalk. When positioned with care, they can complement exterior appearance and present no logical reason for neighbors to object. Obtaining a permit will be determined on "hardship," a need to provide housing for a parent, married or divorced son or daughter, or other relative. A conversion of existing space favors the taxpayer while the energy saved favors the national effort.

An entry door can be installed by removing a window, Illus. 165, or cutting an opening through a blank wall. Select wall space free of plumbing and heating lines. Relocating 110v AC lines presents no big problem.*

Ask your dealer for rough opening size of outside door frame selected. Measure distance X on inside. Go outside. Measure same distance. Draw a line. Add approximately 2¼" for outside door sill, Illus. 165.

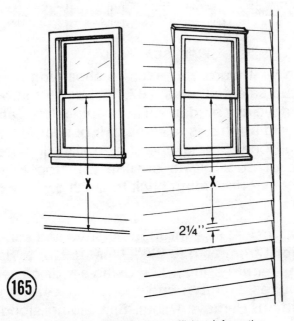

X   X

2¼"

(165)

---

*Book #694 Electrical Repairs Simplified offers sufficient information.

Working from inside, remove window stops and sash, Illus. 143, pry up top casing, then side casing. Remove apron. Knock up and remove sill. Place a short block of 2 x 4 against bottom of window frame and hammer frame out just enough to loosen up nails. Drive frame back and pull out projecting nails. Pry frame out with a wrecking bar.

Since the installation of an outside door requires a scaffold, rent one, Illus. 20, or build one, Illus. 21, using lumber specified in position shown. An adjustable pipe scaffold, Illus. 166, is also available on a rental basis.

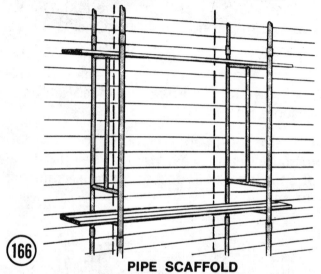

PIPE SCAFFOLD

Saw through wallboard and exterior sheathing and siding alongside stud selected, Illus. 167, 168, down to floor. Saw shoe and remove any stud or sill in opening. Use care not to mar exterior siding that is to remain. If builder left out jack stud A, install one. Frame opening to size door requires. Position top of door frame on line with top of existing windows. Cut exterior siding back to width casings on door frame require.

Working from inside, saw through finished and subflooring and header joist from zero to 2¼", Illus. 169, or to depth sill on door frame requires, Illus. 171. Using a wide chisel, cut to angle sill requires. Plumb frame in opening. Draw outline of casing on siding. Remove frame. Saw siding along drawn

110

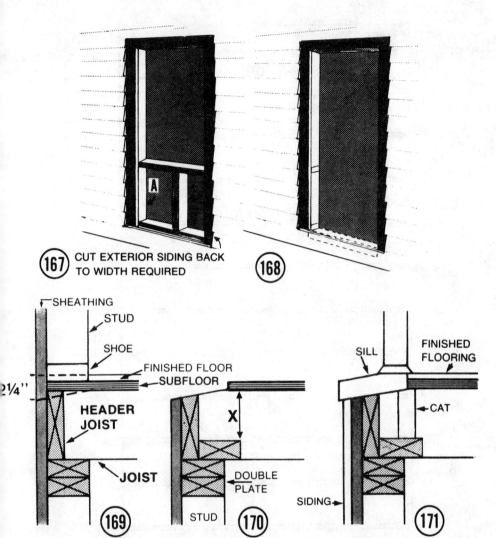

167 CUT EXTERIOR SIDING BACK TO WIDTH REQUIRED

168

SHEATHING
STUD
SHOE
FINISHED FLOOR
SUBFLOOR
2¼"
HEADER JOIST
JOIST

169

X
DOUBLE PLATE
STUD

170

SILL
FINISHED FLOORING
CAT
SIDING

171

line. To support cut edge of flooring, measure distance X, Illus. 170. Cut a 2 x 6 or 2 x 8 to width, length and shape needed for a tight fit. Pry into position to support cut edge of flooring. Toenail or screw through flooring into cat. Install frame and door in opening. Check with level to make certain it's plumb (vertical) and level (horizontal). Check to see that door opens and closes freely. Shim frame in place with pieces of shingle. Drive 10 penny finishing nails through outside casings into studs. Don't drive nails all the way. Use a nailset to protect casings. Countersink heads and fill holes with putty. Calk joint between siding and door casing.

111

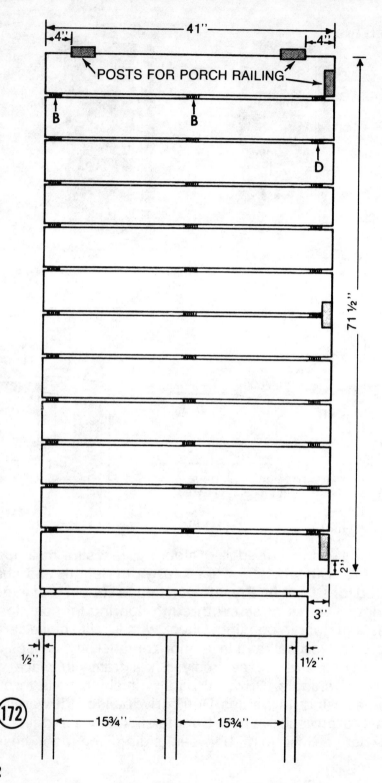

POSTS FOR PORCH RAILING

172

112

CONSTRUCTION OF OUTSIDE STAIRS

As previously suggested, outside stairs can be constructed against side of building, Illus. 2, or built into a sundeck, Illus. 161. Just as the location of a kitchenette will be influenced by existing waste and supply lines, an outside entry door and length of a landing platform or sundeck, will be determined by space available. The landing platform and/or a sundeck permits building stairs wherever it's most convenient.

While directions suggest building a 41 x 71½'' landing, Illus. 172, this size can be altered. Those purchasing precut stair components or assembled stairs should request the retailer to check overall dimensions and advise as to the height and exact location of the base platform, Illus. 173.

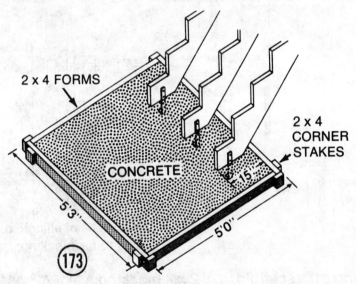

Build a form for base, Illus. 173, using 2 x 4 or 2 x 6, to overall height retailer specifies for precut components or for assembled stairs. Embed 3/16 x 1 x 12'' strap steel, Illus. 176, in concrete, in position each carriage and post requires.

A base should not be less than 5'3'' x 5'0''. It can be constructed to any larger size desired. Excavate to below frost level. Fill with fieldstone. Stake forms in position. Check with level. Measure diagonals to make certain form is square.

113

Paint A,A1,A2,A3,B,C,D, all platform and stair framing with wood preservative after sawing to size required.

A — 2 x 4 x 7¼"
A1— 2 x 4 x 14"
A2— 2 x 4 x 12"
A3— 2 x 4 x 10"

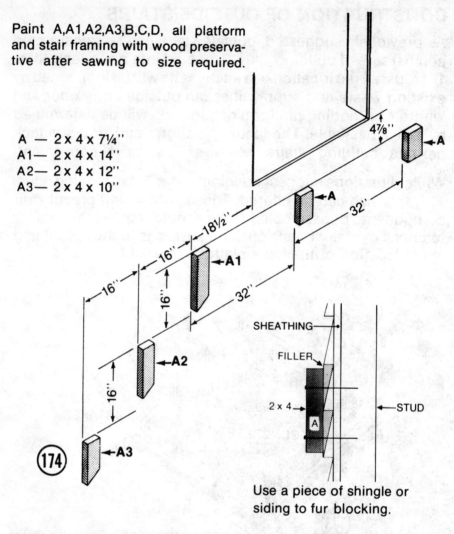

SHEATHING

FILLER

2 x 4

A

STUD

Use a piece of shingle or siding to fur blocking.

Working off a scaffold, nail 2 x 4 blocking A, A1, A2, A3, Illus. 174, in position required. Use pieces of shingle or siding to shim and plumb blocking. Cut blocking to size shown. Apply wood preservative, allow to dry, then paint with color that matches siding. Allow to dry before nailing in place.

Nail a 2 x 8 x 67½" B in position, Illus. 175, 4⅞" below door sill.

Build forms for piers, Illus. 176, in position each post requires, Illus. 178. Dig post holes to a depth below frost level.

114

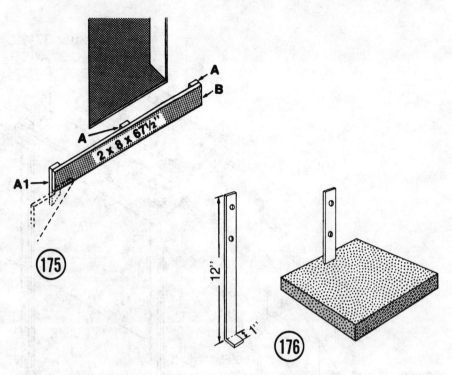

Those who prefer building stairs should use three 2 x 12 x 14' for carriages, Illus. 177. Note 6½'' starting riser, 8'' risers, 9'' treads. When the 2 x 6 tread is placed on starting riser, it makes an 8'' step.

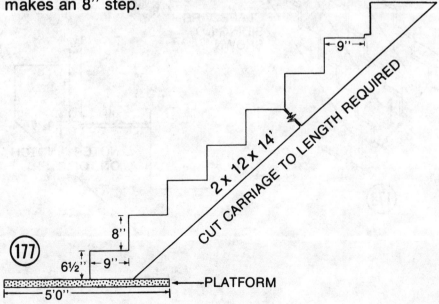

115

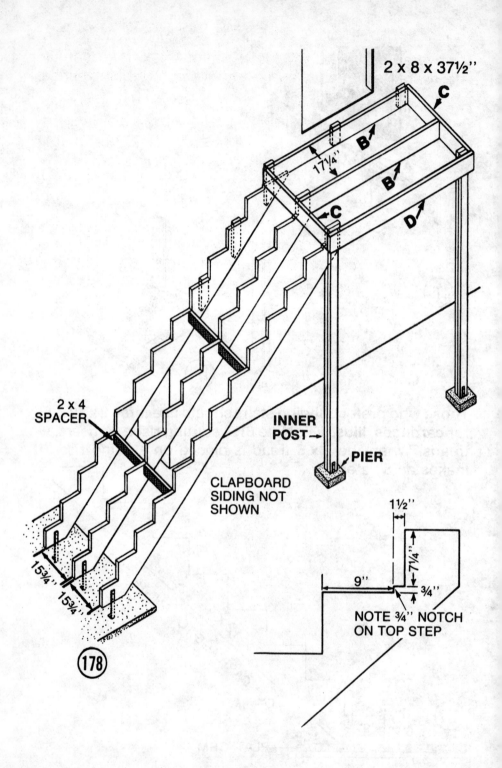

2 x 8 x 37½"

C

B

B

17¼"

C

D

2 x 4
SPACER

INNER
POST→

PIER

CLAPBOARD
SIDING NOT
SHOWN

15¾"

15¾"

1½"

7¼"

9"

¾"

NOTE ¾" NOTCH
ON TOP STEP

(178)

The overall length and width of a landing platform is optional. The overall size specified is the minimum recommended.

The carriage against house butts against bottom of B, Illus. 178, while the other two carriages are cut to length needed to finish flush with top of middle and outside B. All three permit nailing 2 x 8 C in position. Select straight 2 x 12 x 14' free of any loose knots. Fasten steel base straps to side of carriage with two ¼ x 1¼" lag screws.

After nailing 2 x 8 x 67½" B, Illus. 175, in position, cut and nail two 2 x 8 x 37½" C to B. Cut one 2 x 8 x 70½" D. Nail to C. Spike C to another B in position shown with 16 penny nails. Double check C and D to make certain they are level.

Support platform framing level with temporary 2 x 4 bracing. Install two 3½" steel corner columns or double 2 x 4 corner posts on top of concrete piers, Illus. 179. Pier should finish at least 2" above grade to protect bottom of post.

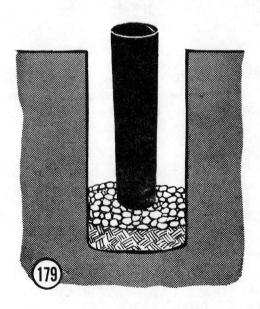

Embed 3/16 x 1 x 12" strap steel in pier if 2 x 4 corner posts are installed. Embed bolts in pier for steel posts.

To locate position of a pier, drop a plumb bob down from corner of CD and dig a hole to below frost level. Throw in some stone and set an 8" foundation form, Illus. 179, in position at height above grade required. Fill and level form using a concrete mix consisting of one part cement to three parts sand, four to five parts gravel. To embed a piece of strap steel in exact position required, place a 2 x 4 temporarily in position. Check with level to make certain it's plumb. Indicate its position in concrete. Embed a steel strap in position. Lag screw it to 2 x 4 post after concrete sets, Illus. 178.

Codes specify Riser x Tread = 72 to 75. An 8" riser x 9" tread = 72. If a 7¾" riser divides equally into overall length of carriage, use a 9½" tread: 7¾ x 9½ = 73+ which is OK. Other codes specify 2R + 1T = 25. Two 8" risers, plus one 9" tread equals 25. If you need to change risers to 7¾": 2R 15½ + 1T 9½ = 25.

Placing carriages on a raised flagstone or slate covered concrete slab built to overall height required helps eliminate any oddball dimension. If length can't be devided by 8", try 7¾ or 7½".

To cut bottom of carriage to angle and height required for a starting riser, place edge of a square in position shown, Illus. 180, with 8 and 9" along top edge. Draw line A.

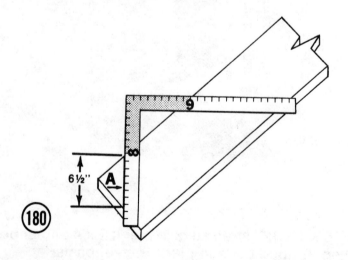

118

Reposition edge of square 6½" down from top and bottom of carriage for first step, Illus. 181, and draw line B.

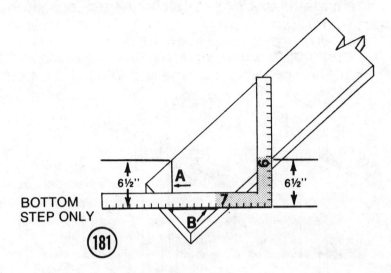

Place square with 8 and 9" in position shown, Illus. 182, and draw lines T and R. Repeat for balance of steps. Cut top of carriage nailed against building to angle that permits nailing to bottom of B. Cut other two carriages to shape shown, Illus. 178. 183.

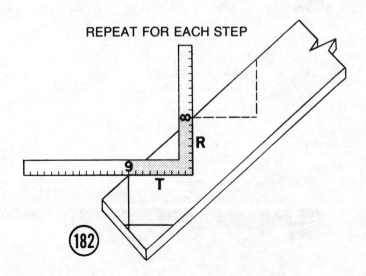

Spike first carriage to A2 and A3, toenail to bottom of B, Illus. 178. Spike center carriage to B, spike C to center carriage. Spike third carriage to 2 x 4 post. Nail 2 x 4 spacers between carriages in position shown.

Cut 2 x 4 inner corner post, Illus. 183, to angle at top and to length required. Toenail to carriage and to outer 2 x 4 post.

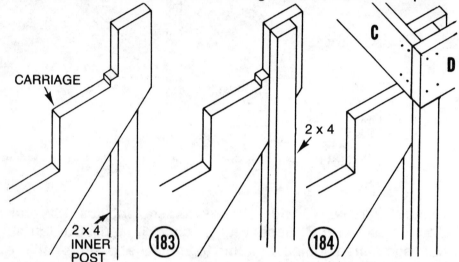

Nail C to carriage and post, Illus. 184; nail through D into post.

Illus. 185 shows 2 x 6 and 2 x 4 tread on carriage against house.

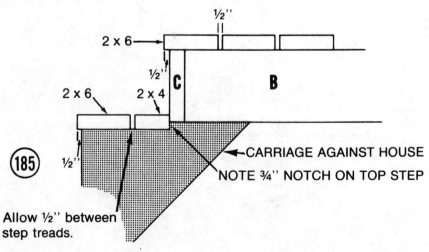

Illus. 172 indicates position of 2 x 6 decking on landing platform, also location of 2 x 4 x 45'' platform railing posts. Cut top of posts and edge of top rail to angle shown full size, Illus. 186.

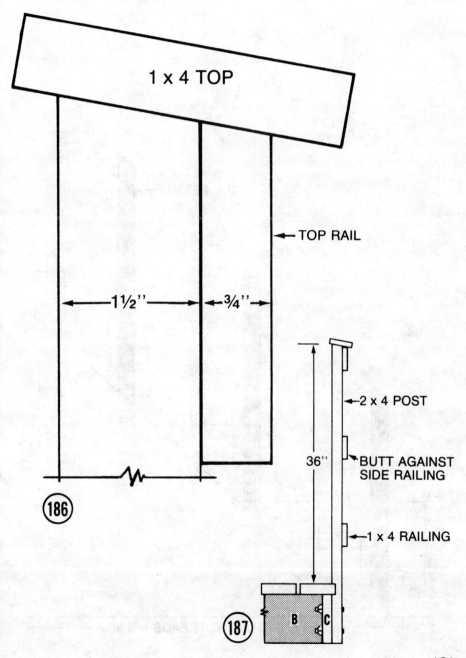

1 x 4 TOP

← TOP RAIL

←—1½''—→ ←—¾''—→

186

2 x 4 POST

36''

BUTT AGAINST SIDE RAILING

1 x 4 RAILING

187   B C

Place post in position indicated, Illus. 172; drill one hole through C or D and bolt post in position with ½ x 4" carriage bolt, Illus. 187, 188. Check with level. When plumb, drill second hole and tighten both bolts.

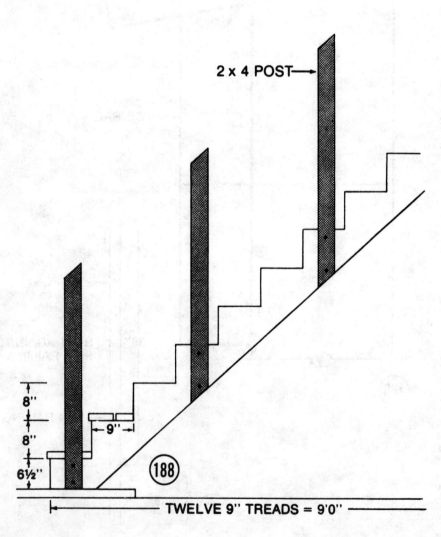

2 x 4 POST⟶

8"

9"

8"

6½"

(188)

TWELVE 9" TREADS = 9'0"

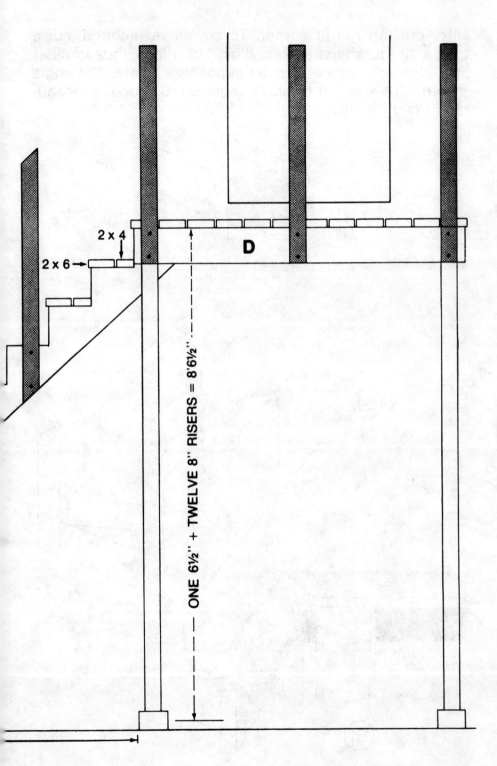

2 x 4

2 x 6

D

ONE 6½" + TWELVE 8" RISERS = 8'6½"

Miter cut top rail at corner. To cut angle required, cut a
1 x 2 x 12" to shape shown, Illus. 189. Place 1 x 2 in miter
box, Illus. 190. Place side rail in position. Cut end to angle
shown. Cut end rail to angle required. Cut both to length
required, Illus. 191.

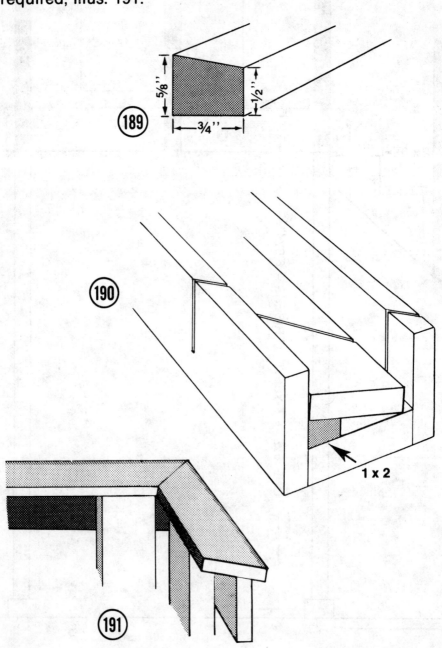

Spacing 2 x 6 platform flooring ½" apart requires twelve 2 x 6 x 41" for platform. Notch first 2 x 6 so it projects ½" over C, Illus. 185, and 1½" over D, Illus. 184. You can cut two 2 x 6 x 41" and one 2 x 6 x 38" from a 2 x 6 x 10'.

Cut top and bottom of 2 x 4 x 45" stair railing posts to angle noted, Illus. 188. Drill one hole and bolt post in position. Plumb with level before drilling second hole through post and carriage.

Cut stair treads 2 x 6 x 38" and 2 x 4 x 38". Space ½" apart. Notch for post. Allow tread to project ½" over carriage against house; 1½" on outside. Nail 2 x 4 and 2 x 6 treads in position indicated, Illus. 185.

Space rails in position indicated, Illus. 192, and nail with 8 penny nails. The top edge of top stair rail on stairs remains square.

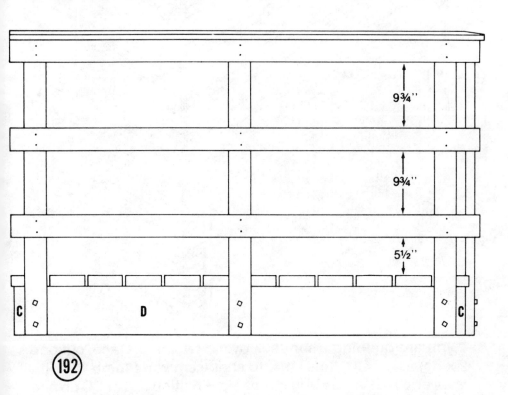

SUNDECK CONSTRUCTION

If your building site provides the space and insures the needed privacy, a sundeck, Illus. 161, adds an enjoyable outdoor area to a second floor apartment. Directions suggest a size that meets most family needs. Build as much sundeck as desired.

Sundeck construction follows same general procedure as outlined for platform. Measure 4⅞" below sill of second floor entry door and snap a level chalk line, Illus. 193. Nail 2 x 4 x 5½" A and 2 x 4 x 12¾" B in position indicated 4⅞" below door sill. B is positioned 5" in from edge of building. Nail as many A and B as length of sundeck requires. Cut and nail C in position shown.

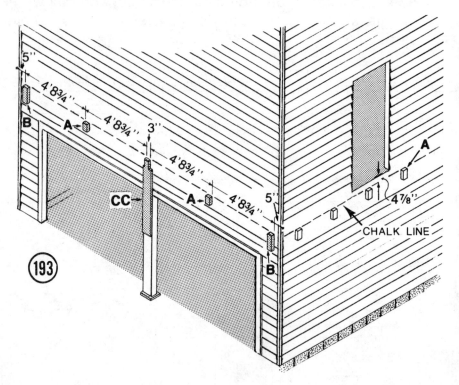

If you are building a sundeck over a two car garage, cut one 2 x 6 x 51¼" CC, Illus. 194, to shape shown. Plumb CC with level and nail in position indicated. Position top of CC on line with A and B, Illus. 193.

After cutting to length and shape required, paint with wood preservative. Allow to dry, then nail in place. Plumb with level before nailing into studs. Use 10 or 16 penny nails.

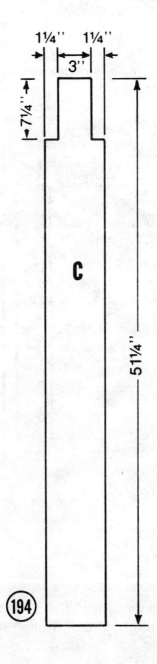

Cut 2 x 8 x 5'10" D, Illus. 195. Nail D flush with bottom of B. Check with level. Brace with temporary 2 x 4 post. The 2 x 8 nailed flush with bottom of B are girders. The 2 x 8 DD, nailed to top of CC are headers, Illus. 196. Install two D at left end, one on each side of B. Do the same at right end.

D — 2 x 8 x 5'10"

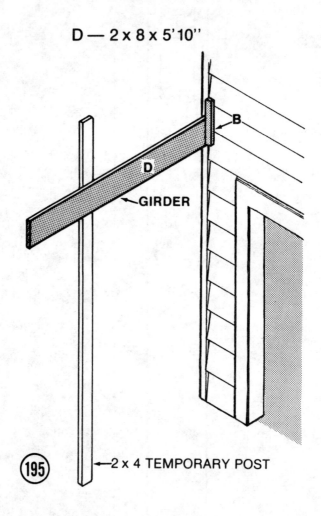

GIRDER

B

D

2 x 4 TEMPORARY POST

(195)

Saw a 2 x 4 x 5'10" down center of 3½" width. Nail 1½ x 1¾" E flush with bottom edge of DD, Illus. 196. Check DD with level. Support with temporary 2 x 4 brace.

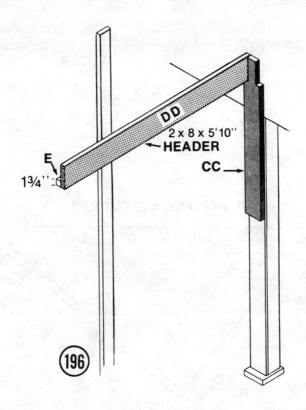

DD

2 x 8 x 5'10"
HEADER

CC

E

1¾"

(196)

Nail 1½ x 1½ x 5½" filler blocks in position shown, Illus. 197.

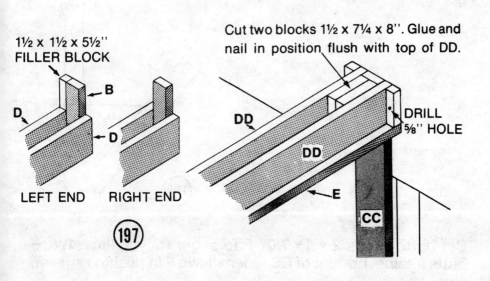

1½ x 1½ x 5½"
FILLER BLOCK

B

D

D

LEFT END   RIGHT END

(197)

Cut two blocks 1½ x 7¼ x 8". Glue and
nail in position flush with top of DD.

DD

DD

DRILL
⅝" HOLE

E

CC

129

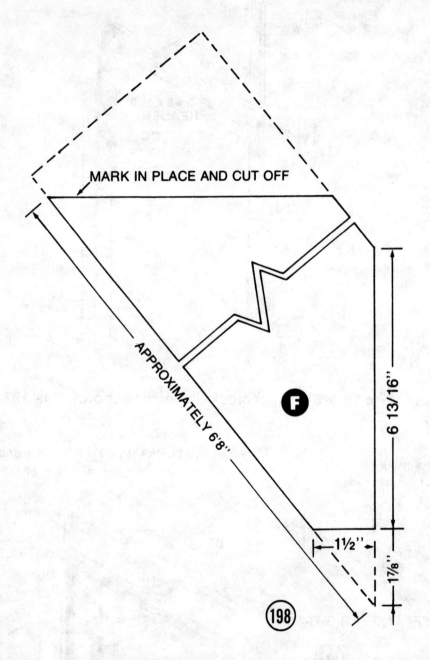

MARK IN PLACE AND CUT OFF

APPROXIMATELY 6'8''

6 13/16''

1½''

1⅛''

F

(198)

Cut bottom of a 2 x 6 x 7'0'' F to angle shown, Illus. 198. F butts against bottom of CC. Toenail two F in position shown, Illus. 199.

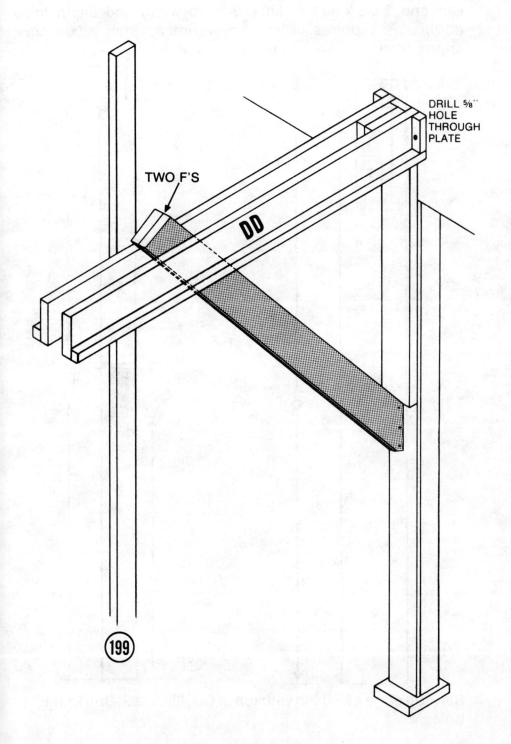

DRILL ⅝"
HOLE
THROUGH
PLATE

TWO F'S

DD

Cut one 2 x 6 x 50" K, Illus. 200, to width and depth the double F requires. Dimensions noted, Illus. 200, are approximate. Spike K in place, Illus. 201.

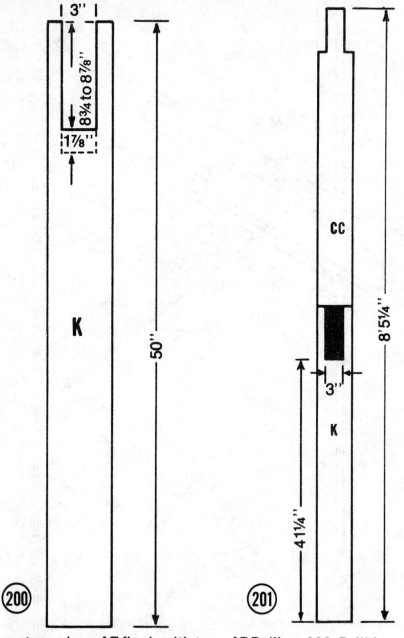

Saw top edge of F flush with top of DD, Illus. 202. Drill four ½" holes.

Cut two 2 x 4 x 7¼'' filler blocks. Apply glue, insert and nail in place. Bolt DD and F, Illus. 202, with four ½ x 8'' bolts. Tighten nuts on bolts.

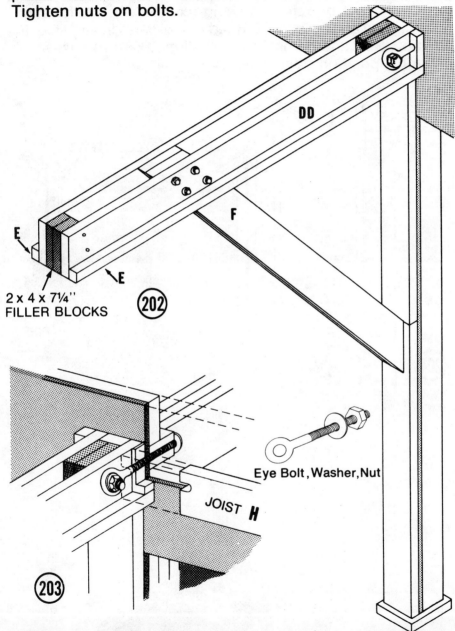

DD

F

E

E

2 x 4 x 7¼''
FILLER BLOCKS

(202)

Eye Bolt, Washer, Nut

JOIST H

(203)

Drill ⅝'' holes through filler blocks and plate. Insert ⅝ x 10'' eye bolts, Illus. 203. Drill hole through DD and fasten eyebolts in position.

133

To locate center for a pier, drop a plumb bob 2¼" from end of girder, Illus. 204. Dig to depth below frost level. Position an 8" form, Illus. 179, or build one using 1 x 8. Pour a pier for each post slightly above grade. Embed a steel strap in each pier in position permanent post requires, Illus. 205. If you use steel columns, position bolts, Illus. 206.

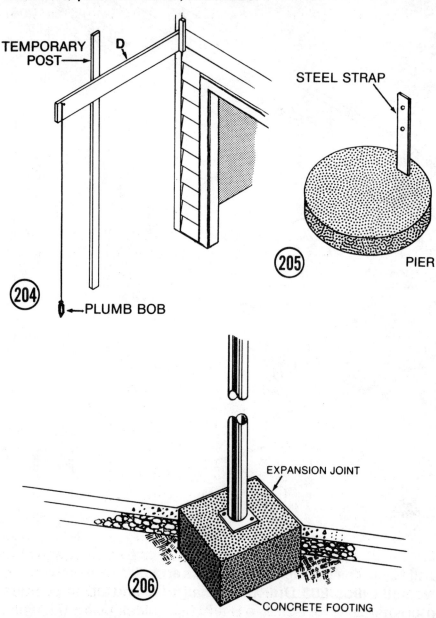

TEMPORARY POST

D

STEEL STRAP

PIER

(205)

(204) PLUMB BOB

EXPANSION JOINT

(206)

CONCRETE FOOTING

After pier has set up (allow three days), measure exact height required for post. Cut three 2 x 4 to length needed to finish flush with top of D, Illus. 207, 208. Glue and nail together. Plumb post in two directions. Nail through D into post. Lag screw steel strap to bottom. Due to the variation in concrete work, measure and cut posts to height each requires to hold girders level. Cut and nail inside D in position, Illus. 208.

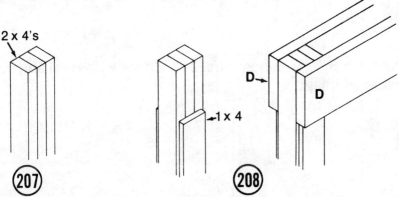

Cut 1 x 4 to height needed to butt against bottom of D, Illus. 208. Recess these ½" from edge and nail to both sides of each post.

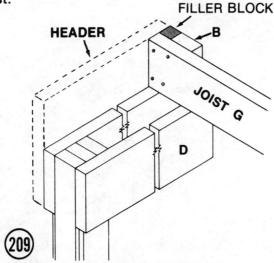

Cut five 2 x 6 joists G to length required to butt against DD and finish flush with filler block, Illus. 209, 211. Notch end to receive eyebolt, Illus. 203. Toenail to D and DD in position shown, Illus. 210. Spike to B and filler block using 16d nails.

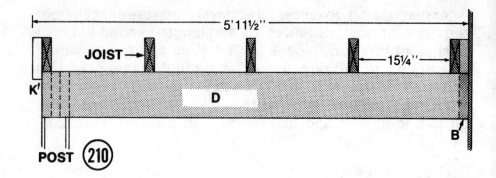

Cut 2 x 8 x 5'10'' header, Illus. 211. Check with level and nail to ends of joists.

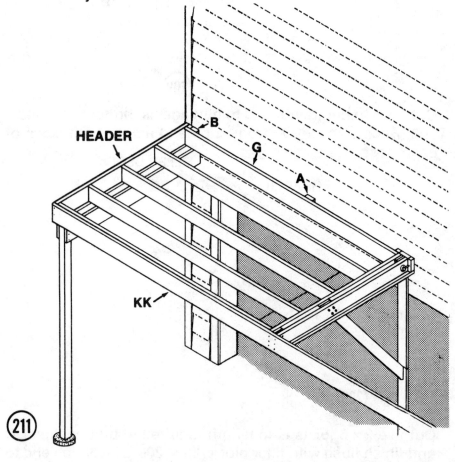

Cut 2 x 6 x 16' joist HH to length required so it can be nailed to post. Spike HH to each A, Illus. 193, and to post D, Illus. 212.

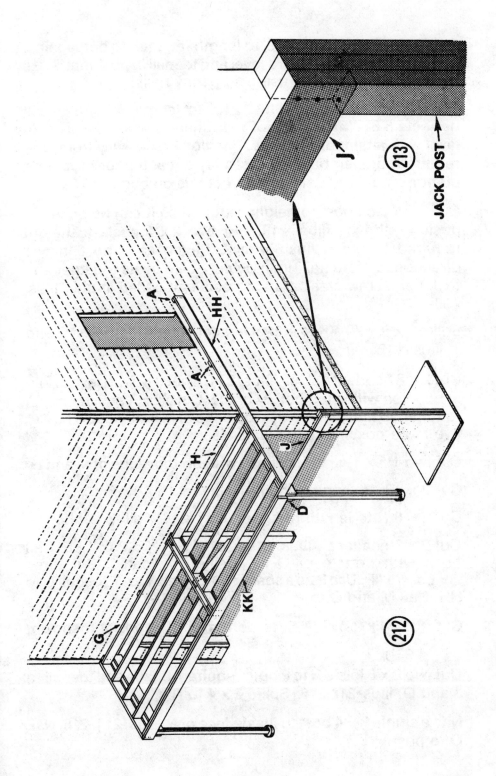

JACK POST →

J

213

A

HH

A

H

J

D

KK

G

212

137

Cut four joists H, Illus. 212, to length required to butt against DD, HH. Check each with a level and toenail in position. Spike HH to ends of joists H using 16 penny nails.

Cut 2 x 6 x 16' joist J, Illus. 212, to length required so it projects 5'8½" from face of HH. Check J with a level. Hold level with a temporary brace. Position brace away from area required for stair base. You can lay out and pour form for a platform now or later. Note directions on page 113.

Cut 2 x 4 jack post to height required so it can be nailed in position shown, Illus. 213. Cut two 2 x 4 posts to height required to finish flush with J. Plumb each post in two directions before nailing in place. Spike posts together and to J. Lag screw steel strap to posts embedded in pier, Illus. 205.

Spike 2 x 8 x 20' KK to end of header, Illus. 211, to joist G and J, Illus. 212.

Cut 2 x 8 header M 5'10", Illus. 214. Check M with level. Hold in position with a temporary brace. Cut a 2 x 4 post to length required to finish flush with top edge of M. Nail post to M. Cut two more posts. Nail in place.

Cut two 1½ x 1¾" E. Nail flush with bottom edge of M and O.

Cut 2 x 8 L to length required. Nail to J.

Cut 2 x 8 N to length required, Illus. 216. Nail to LJM.

Cut 2 x 8 header O, Illus. 214. Cut 1½ x 1¾ x 29½" EE. Nail flush with bottom of O in position indicated. Cut three 2 x 6 x 4'4" P. Use P as a spacer for O. Nail N to O, toenail O to HH. Nail M and O to P.

Cut a 2 x 4 x 29½". Nail to bottom of J in position shown, Illus. 215.

Cut two 2 x 6 joists R to length required. Space and toenail to J and O, Illus. 214, 216. Spike 2 x 4 to R.

Nail a single 2 x 4 post to inside face of N, Illus. 214, 216. Nail O to post.

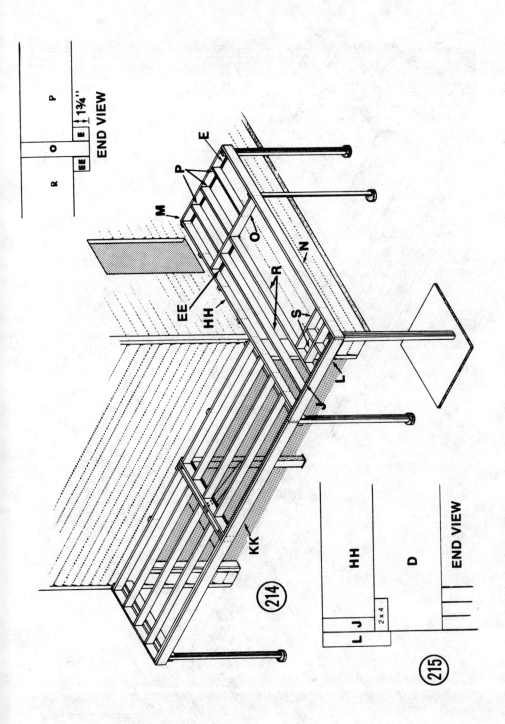

END VIEW

13¾"

214

215

HH

D

END VIEW

139

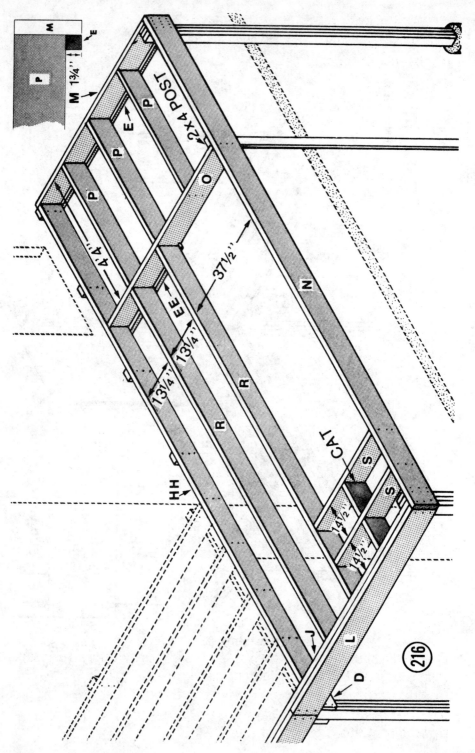

M

E

M 1¾"

P

E

P

P

P

2X4 POST

O

4X4

EE

37½"

N

1¾"

1¾"

R

R

CAT

S

S

HH

4½"

4½"

J

L

D

216

140

Cut two 2 x 6 S to length required. Nail N to S, toenail S to R. Cut 2 x 6 cat. Nail S to cat, toenail cat to J. Nail second S in position indicated, Illus. 214, 216.

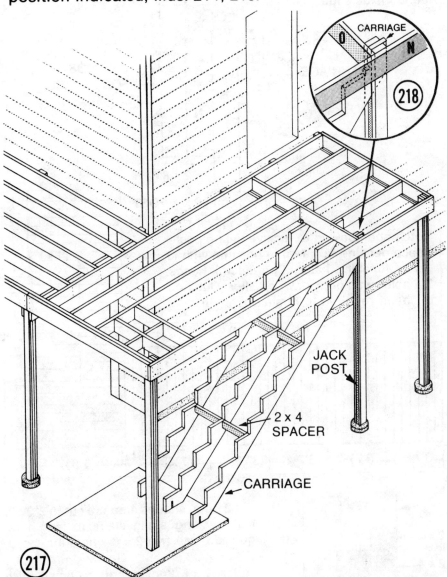

Cut three carriages following directions previously outlined. Nail carriage to post. Nail O to carriage, Illus. 217. Cut a jack post to angle of carriage. Toenail to bottom of carriage. Spike to outer post. Cut a third 2 x 4 post to height of O. Nail to jack post. Nail O to each post, Illus. 218.

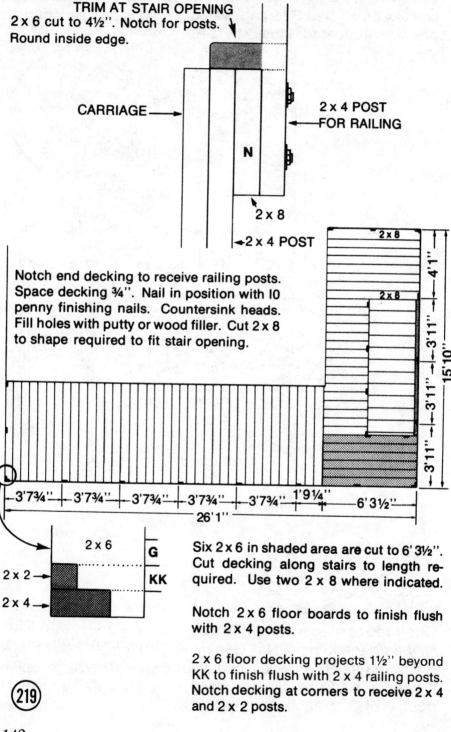

TRIM AT STAIR OPENING
2 x 6 cut to 4½". Notch for posts.
Round inside edge.

CARRIAGE

2 x 4 POST
FOR RAILING

N

2 x 8

2 x 4 POST

Notch end decking to receive railing posts.
Space decking ¾". Nail in position with I0
penny finishing nails. Countersink heads.
Fill holes with putty or wood filler. Cut 2 x 8
to shape required to fit stair opening.

2 x 8

2 x 8

4'1"

3'11"

3'11"

3'11"

15'10"

3'7¾" — 3'7¾" — 3'7¾" — 3'7¾" — 3'7¾" — 1'9¼" — 6'3½"
26'1"

2 x 6   G
2 x 2 →   KK
2 x 4 →

Six 2 x 6 in shaded area are cut to 6' 3½".
Cut decking along stairs to length required. Use two 2 x 8 where indicated.

Notch 2 x 6 floor boards to finish flush
with 2 x 4 posts.

2 x 6 floor decking projects 1½" beyond
KK to finish flush with 2 x 4 railing posts.
Notch decking at corners to receive 2 x 4
and 2 x 2 posts.

(219)

Spike other two carriages to joists P, Illus. 217. Nail O to carriages, nail 2 x 4 spacers.

Cut and nail stair treads following directions on page 120. Stair treads for sundeck are cut 39" in length. This allows 1½" overhang on both sides.

If you plan on enclosing area under stairs for a tool house, pave the entire area including stair platform.

Cut 2 x 4 posts for sundeck and stair railing to length and angle shown, Illus. 186, 187, 192. Place in position indicated, Illus. 219. Keep bottom of post flush with KK, Illus. 220, 161. Drill one hole and bolt post with ½ x 6" bolt. Plumb each post with a level. Drill a second hole. Add a 2 x 2 post at corners, Illus. 219.

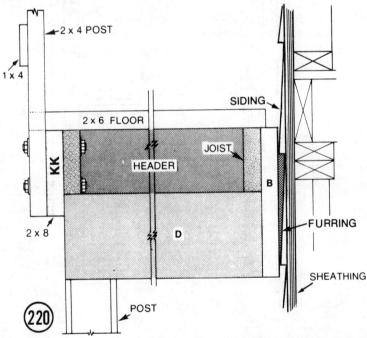

If local codes require additional support for stairs, cut a jack post to height required. Toenail to carriage. Cut an outer post to angle and height required and use it in place of stair railing post, Illus. 161.

Complete siding. Calk all joints around window and door frames.

143

TO REPLACE OR INSTALL A NEW WINDOW

If you decide to replace a window or install additional ones, select a matching size and style. Always position a new window in line, vertically and horizontally with others.

To ascertain size, measure A and B, Illus. 221. If you are replacing an exact size window, always measure A at three points, B at two points.

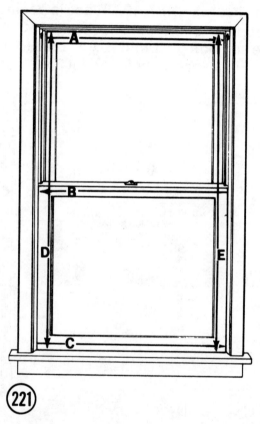

Using a chisel, pry out side stops A, Illus. 222, then top stop. Remove lower sash. Cut sash cords. Allow weights in older windows to drop down.

Remove parting stop, Illus. 223, then top sash. Again cut cords. Remove pulleys. These are usually fastened with screws.

144

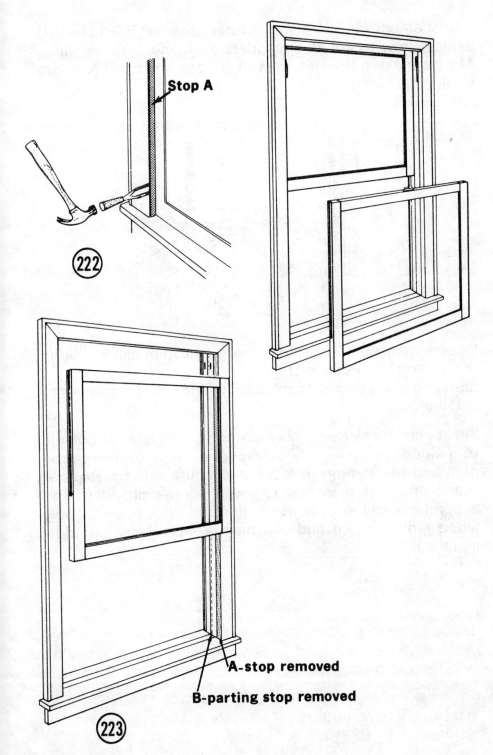

Stop A

(222)

A-stop removed

B-parting stop removed

(223)

145

Replacement window manufacturers provide directions that explain how to adjust expanders on frame to fill opening. Always make a dry run. Test fit window in opening before applying calking.

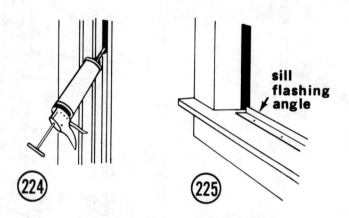

sill
flashing
angle

Directions usually suggest running a bead of calking along inside edge of outside trim, Illus. 224. Some replacement manufacturers provide a sill flashing angle that is screwed to sill, Illus. 225.

Tilt replacement frame over sill angle and against outside trim. Check with level in two directions. If replacement can be plumbed in opening, remove and apply calking. Replace frame and fasten in position with screws provided. The expander is anchored to trim with sheet metal screws. Apply wood molding trim and you have a replacement window installed.

REPAIRING DAMAGED SASH

In many cases you can salvage even damaged sash by removing and regluing. The sash in a double hung window is held in place with stops A, Illus. 222, and with a parting stop B, Illus. 223. The stops A are usually nailed in place with 3 penny finishing nails. Start at bottom of stop, or alongside any nail you see. Insert a 1" or 1¼" putty knife between stop and trim and pry up stop. Only pry a little at a time. If the stop doesn't budge, use a nailset. Drive nails through stop. If a putty knife is too flexible, use a flat chisel. Remove side stop, then top and parting stop. Plan on replacing stops if you have trouble removing them.

Carefully disconnect sash cord or chain. Tack end of cord temporarily to the trim. Replace sash cord where needed. Your hardware and lumber dealer sells replacement chain, Illus. 226. Cut to length needed.

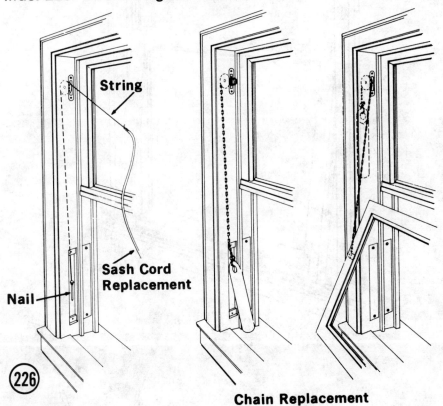

String

Sash Cord
Replacement

Nail

226

Chain Replacement

147

If existing sash only needs regluing, remove stops. Place sash in position noted with a broom handle or 1 x 2 across frame, Illus. 227. Thin down waterproof glue and soak the corners. Apply clamp to hold frame square while glue sets. Fill holes, nicks or breaks with a wood filler. Sandpaper smooth. When painted you'll have difficulty finding the repair.

clamp

1 x 2 →

227

Another way to repair a sash without removing same is with a wood wedge, Illus. 229, and metal corner plates, Illus. 227, 228. Remove stops. Apply glue to crack. Drive wedge to tighten sash. Use care not to crack glass. While the wedge holds sash, fasten 2 or 2½'' flat corner brackets in position shown.

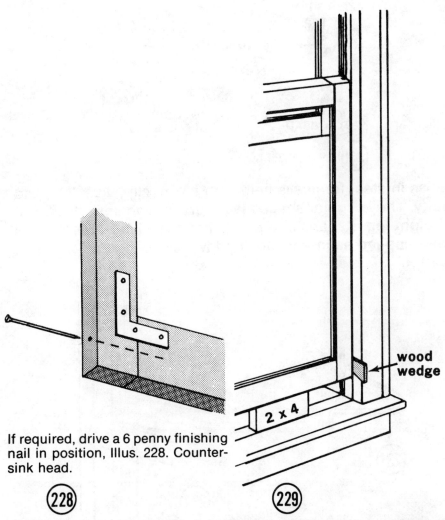

If required, drive a 6 penny finishing nail in position, Illus. 228. Countersink head.

228

229

wood wedge

2 x 4

Heat from a propane torch can be used to remove old putty prior to installing new glass. A street level window that's vulnerable to breakage should be glazed with non-breakable acrylic. While more expensive than glass, its lifespan and safety factor more than warrant the cost.

FACTS ABOUT GLAZING

Glass in a wood frame is usually held in place with triangular glazier points and putty, Illus. 230; or a wood molding called a glass bead or putty bead.

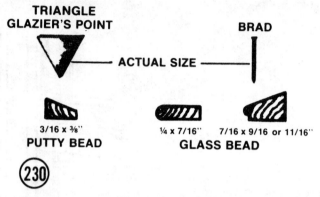

TRIANGLE
GLAZIER'S POINT

BRAD

—— ACTUAL SIZE ——

3/16 x ⅜"
PUTTY BEAD

¼ x 7/16"   7/16 x 9/16 or 11/16"
GLASS BEAD

230

Glass in steel frames is held with a wire clip, Illus. 231, and putty. The irregular shaped leg A presses against glass. The straight leg B snaps into a hole in frame, Illus. 232. Putty is then applied as in a wood window.

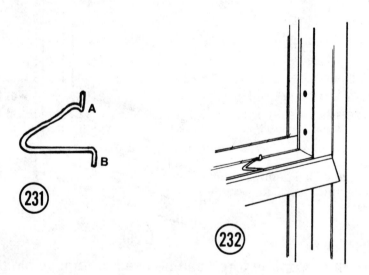

231

232

Some steel sashes were manufactured with a steel molding. This is screwed in the same position as a glass bead.

Aluminum window manufacturers use the kind of spring clip shown in Illus. 233. The shaped head fits under edge of glass, Illus. 234, 235. The legs are spread to butt against frame. Most glaziers use one close to the ends, one every 16 to 18''. The putty is then applied and beveled.

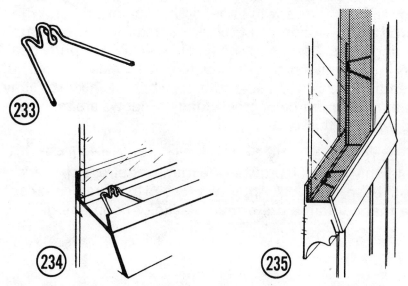

Many aluminum window manufacturers set glass in a plastic or neoprene gasket, Illus. 236. This can be pried out and reused. Since this may be difficult to replace, use care not to damage. Always use the same thickness glass as originally installed. Do not use putty, or a putty bed with this gasket. When replacing, apply vaseline to help slide gasket in groove.

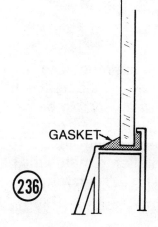

GASKET

Always remove broken glass and inspect old putty for clips. Always note how many and where these clips were installed.

After removing broken glass, scrape frame carefully to remove bits of old putty. If putty is hard, apply heat using a torch or soldering iron. When area is clean, paint rabbet in a wood window frame with linseed oil or paint primer. When dry, roll out a ribbon of putty and spread it thin over area receiving glass. Use a putty knife. This is called a "putty bed" and is important. It provides a cushion that seals out cold air, prevents windows from rattling, while it absorbs any irregularities in frame or glass. Many windows are manufactured without this bed.

Don't spread the putty bed too thick. This creates globs. Spread only as much putty as the frame requires to provide a smooth base, Illus. 237. Apply a putty bed to all frames except those that contain a preformed plastic or neoprene gasket.

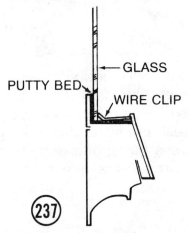

GLASS

PUTTY BED

WIRE CLIP

237

Always cut glass to size of opening, less ⅛" in overall width and height. This provides 1/16" clearance all around. If you have no confidence in your ability to measure the glass area, cut a cardboard pattern full size of opening less ⅛". Note how pattern fits into opening with just 1/16" clearance all around. Ask your glass retailer to match the pattern. Tell him you have already allowed for ⅛" clearance and he'll consider you a pro.

WOOD WINDOW — PUTTY

Press glass into putty bed. Use edge of a chisel or screwdriver to press or tap glazier points in frame about 2" from corners of a small window; and every 10" from corner in a larger window. Glazier points need only be driven in about ½ their overall height, Illus. 238. Use care not to scratch glass. Never replace glazier points, Illus. 230, in previous hole.

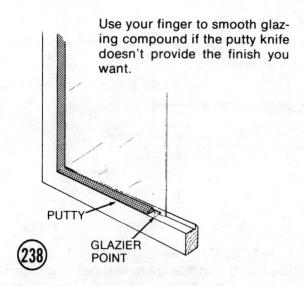

Use your finger to smooth glazing compound if the putty knife doesn't provide the finish you want.

PUTTY

(238)

GLAZIER POINT

Knead putty to make it pliable, then roll it into long strips about pencil thickness. Place it in rabbet, press and bevel with a putty knife, Illus. 238. The linseed oil or paint primer permits putty to bond to frame.

Allow putty to dry about a week before applying paint. When painting, seal putty to glass with a hairline of paint on glass.

WOOD WINDOW — GLASS BEAD

Remove all broken glass. Glass bead is usually nailed in place with small brads. Note where bead was nailed and insert a wood chisel, wide screwdriver or narrow putty knife in center, Illus. 239, preferably alongside a brad. Carefully raise bead, pull brads using pliers wherever nailed.

ONLY REMOVE INSIDE BEAD

(239)

Carefully lift out inside bead at mitered corners. Never remove outside bead. Scrape away old paint and putty. Paint area with linseed oil. Spread a putty bed as outlined previously. Replace glass and renail bead along short sides first. Bow to insert longer lengths in position. Make new holes when renailing. Countersink heads of brads. Fill old and new nail holes with putty, then paint.

Because of warpage or paint build-up, the bead in many old frames is sometimes difficult to remove without damage. If damage occurs, repair with putty after replacing bead. When repainted, it's hard to find where the chisel scarred molding. Or install a new glass bead. If the original glass was installed without a bed of putty, you will find it necessary to file mitered ends of bead to shorten overall length. Always maintain angle of miter.

STEEL SASH

Replacing a window in a steel sash requires special clips, Illus. 231, 232. The broken glass and old putty is removed. It's frequently necessary to use a propane torch to loosen old putty on a metal cash. Again apply a thin bed of putty before setting glass in place. Press one leg of spring clip against glass, the other leg snaps into predrilled holes in sash, Illus. 232. Putty is then applied as previously described.

If steel sash has metal glass beads, these are screwed to frame. Spray screws with Liquid Wrench, insert screwdriver in screw slot, hit screwdriver lightly with hammer. This frequently jars screws loose.

ALUMINUM WINDOWS

Glass in these windows is held in place with clips, Illus. 233, and putty. Again remove glass and putty. Apply putty bed and replace glass. Press clips into place. Place head under edge while legs press against frame. Bevel putty to width frame requires.

Always purchase double strength glass for larger windows, single strength for smaller windows.

INDEX TO MONEY-SAVING REPAIRS, IMPROVEMENTS, PATTERNS AND BOOKS
(Number designates EASI-BILD Pattern or Book)

Acoustic Ceiling 615,665,685
Add-a-Room 609
Adhesives,use of 623, ceramic tile 606
Air Cooler, window 135
Air Conditioner,framing 632,665,685,773
Airplane,see toy
Alarm,devices 695
  bell , fire
  automatic telephone alarm
Anchor bolts 84,609,617,663,697
Antiquing 623,761
Apron,window 605,609,679,685
Asphalt Roofing 696
Asphalt Tile,how to lay 615,665
Attic Modernization 665,603,773
  built-in lighting 694
Baby Cradle 773
Ballcock,toilet 675
Bars 690
  buffet 718
  cabinet 189,690
  colonial tavern 612
  corner 690
  playroom 490,690
  radio & Hi-Fi 490
  revolving shelf 508
  room divider 658
  sink 490
  storage 634
  table 140
  TV bar 690
  wall 612
  wine storage 634
Barbecue 73,316,668
Barge boat 77
Batter boards 609,631,632,663,679,680
Basement,house 632
Basement Modernization 615
  drapery 627; electrical wiring 694
  entry 615; luminous ceilings 694
  waterproofing 617
Baseboard 605,609
Bathroom Accessories
  bathtub beauty bar 327
  bathtub repairs 675 ,682
  lavatory enclosure 158,606
  medicine chest repairs 694
  radiator enclosure 544
  shelf 4,5,8,557
  towel rack 29; vanity 606
Bathroom Installation 682,685
  bathtub,lavatory,medicine cabinet
  plumbing wall
  prefab bathroom unit, shower, toilet
Beds and Bunks
  colonial 68,761
  double-deck 87,771
  headboard 126
  houseboat 676
  studio 633,623
  under bed storage 634
Bell alarm 695
  installation 694
Benches
  cobbler's 102A,586,761
  colonial 23,94,309,586
  dining 307; fireside 23,761
  lawn 57,325,307; peasant 57
  work 15,568,576,672,677
Bi Fold Door, closet 634

Birdhouses, feeders 669
  bluebird 110,669
  feeder 9,669,677
  martin 669; Swedish 10
  wrens 11,111,102B,669
Blackboard
  kitchen message center 313,578
  play table 117
Bluebird house 110,669
Boats
  barge or pram 77
  cartop float 247
  houseboat 676
  kayak 317
  rowboat 77,85
  sail,centerboard 194
  sail scooter 248
  surfboard 247
  toy 60,67,72
Body harness 674,696
Bolts, anchor, see anchor bolts
Bookcases 664,658,634,690
  desk 18; hanging 21
  record comb. 192
  room divider 658; valance 271
  wall-to-wall 612,658,664,719
  window 271
Bookends 102A
Bow window 609
Breezeway
  how to build 910
  how to screen 613
Bricklaying 668,674
  walls, walks, terraces,
  veneering, mortar mixes
Bridging 609,613,697
Broomcloset 156,634
Buildings, see Garage,Homes,Houses
Built-In
  bookcase 664
  closet 634
  counter range 608,658
  cornice 627
  hi-fi 612
  lighting 694
  record storage 192,436,634,658
  refrigerator 608,658
  sewing center 634
  sink 608,658
  storage units 634
  traverse track 627
  wall oven 608,658
  wall-to-wall 612,634,664
Buffet, bar 718
  dining 138,718
Bulletin Board 93 607
Bungalow, see cabins
Bunks, see beds
Burglary alarm installation 695
Cabinets
  bar 189,490
  built-in 658; cleaning utensil 156
  contemporary 658; corner 38
  display 159M,607,627; end table 141
  fishing rod 130,630;freestanding 658
  furniture 658,634; gun 130,266,630
  hi-fi 272,612; ironing board 615
  kitchen 201,242,243,244,
        245,246,608,658
  pole 658

record 192,436,658; train board 190
wall hanging 24; wall oven 608,658
wall-to-wall 191,192,193,608,
        634,658,664,719
  wine storage 608,634
Cabins, cottages 51,84,91,632,684
Camper 594
Cane Webbing 623
Caning 623
Canopy 305,607
Canned goods storage 770,608,634
Canvas Deck 613
Cape Cod House 514
Carpeting 683
Carport 273,680
Casement window 609,613
Casing 609,605
Cat entry 724,751
Caulking also calking 613,682
Cavy Cage 751
Cedar Room 265,634
Ceiling joists 609,613,615,632
Ceiling,suspended 615,665,685
Ceiling trim plate 674
Ceramic tile
  how to lay 606
Chairs
  child's lawn 132,754
  interior 92,306
  lawn 32,56,169,311,322R,548,754
  repair 623; refinish 623
  reupholstery 623
Chaise 78,169,312,324R,754
Chalk line 617,697
Charts, reference; drill bits 76l,753
  glue 623
  kitchen equipment 608
  lumber conversion—lineal ft.
    to board ft. 623
  metric conversion 606,607,677,751,761
  molding 623
  nails 634,627; screws 623,658
Chest,see wardrobe
  blanket 37,761,962
  cabinet 129
  storage 634
  tool 71,576,672
  toy and storage 37,65,962
  wardrobe 723
Chicken house 14
Children's Furniture
  blackboard,message center 313,578
  blackboard table 117,771
  bookcases & shelves 18,21,192,664
  book ends 102B; bulletin board 93
  bunks and beds 68,87,771
  desk 18,537; door stops 102B
  giraffe clothes tree 34,771
  headboard 126; lawn chair 132
  lamps 98; magazine rack 25,920
  picture frames 97; playtable 117
  record and hi-fi cabinets 192,272,436
  shoe shine box 45; shoe rack 345
  step stool 353,771
  storage cabinets 138,634
  storage chest 37,65,962
  telephone shelf 313
  TV tables 16,925
  trainboard 190,677
  wall decorations 102B,539,580,581
  wall shelves 4,6,31,35,102B,159M,578

Child's Playhouse 148,649
Chimes, Swedish door 561,677
Chimney 91,910,674,696
  construction 674
  cricket 674,696
  flashing 674,696
  flat roof 674
  prefabricated 632
  slip section 674
Christmas Displays
  angel 769
  angel banner 670
  animated 762,764
  camels 410C
  candy cane 435
  carolers 331
  choir boys 562
  fireplace mantel 768
  giant cards, posters, murals
    149,331,540,560,562,592,
    762,764,769,942A,942B
  illuminated 560,562,592,764,767,769,694
  indoor decorations 310,767,768
  madonna 149,540,767
  nativity 310(table top)
          410(life size)
  noel greeting 531
  reindeer & sleigh 433,434,764
  santa 431,575,762
Christmas Displays
  window painting 149
  wise men greeting 560
  wreath 767
Cistern, how to build 617
Clamps 623
Clapboard, siding 609,613,631
Closets 634,773
Clothes Tree 34
Clothing storage 634
Cobbler's bench 102A,586,761
Coffee tables, see table
Colonial
  bench 23,761; cabinet 627
  candleholder 559
  cobblers bench 102A,586,761
  corner cupboard 38; cradle-rocker 773
  cupola 589; doll cradle 773
  furniture 761
  hutch cabinet 270,761
  planters 102A,933; table-bench 94,761
  tavern bar 612
  wall shelves 2,24; weathervane 524
  window valance 1,27,30,157,627
Concrete & Masonry
  barbecue 73,316,668,674
  bricklaying 668,674
  chimney 674
  block layout stick 617
  colors 617
  culverts, curbs 732
  decorator blocks 582
  floors, garage & basement 273,615,617
    632,663,680,697
  footprint stepping stones 96
  foundations & footings 84,86,113,
    609,613,617,632,663,697
  how-to-book 617
  mixing 617
  patio floor 591,631,606
  piles 567

Concrete & Masonry
  repairs 617
  steps 617
  tools 617
  waterproofing 617
  work simplified 617
Contemporary Furniture 658
Cooler, attic air 135
Cornice
  how to build 612,627
  install traverse rod 627
Corner cabinet 38,242
Cot, string bed 623,676
Cottages, see homes
Counter
  serving 80,243
  sink 608,658
  tops 608,658
Cradle, baby 761, 773
Cricket 696
Cupola, colonial 589,609,680
Day Bed, 633,623
Deck 631
Desks 18,139,537,542,608,658
Diagonal bracing 609,613,632
Dining, bench 307
  buffet 138
  table 94,95,137,554
Displays, see Christmas displays
  case 159M,607
Dividers, room 128,263,308,605,
    608,658,930
  outdoor privacy 607,617,631,668,937
Dog House 28,751
Doll carriage 59,61
  cradle 753,773
Dollhouse 33,596,753
  furniture 753
Door
  bi-fold 634
  chimes 561
  decorate with plysculpture 704
  garage 86
  glass sliding 613
  how to install 608,609,613,615,631,658
  modernizing 623
  remove 608
  outside entry 615
  sliding 658
  storage 634
Dormer,how to build 603,665,773
Double hung windows 609,613,685
Drain, clogged 675
Drainage Tile 617,615
Drapery 627
  how to make 627
  traverse track installation 627,605
Drawers
  how to build 608,658
Driveway
  culverts, curbs 732
  markers 438,587
Dry Well 617
Easel, artists 555
Edging Tool
  concrete 617
Electric Light Gardening 611,694
Electrical Repairs 694
  wiring, built-in lighting 694
End tables 99,127,141,925

Enclosures
  books, see built-in
  brooms, mops 156,634
  chimney 674
  hi-fi and record 192,272,436,612
  ironing board 615; lavatory 158,606
  lighting 694; porch 613
  pots and pans 578; radiator 544
  refrigerator 608,658
  sink 41,158; trains 190
  truck body camper 594
  wall oven 608,658
  window, see valance
Entry, outdoors 615,617
Excavating 663
Expansion joint 613
Expansion plug 613,615,631,658
Express wagon 40
Exterior Siding 609,663,696
Fan, window 135
Farmyard animals 79,83
Fascia 609,613,632,663,696
Faucet
  repairs 675
  replacement 675
  seat 675
Feeders, bird 9,669
Fences 668,607
  rail 941,607
  privacy 937,607,668
  Williamsburg 315,607
Ferrule 682
Fireplace 73,316,668,674
  Christmas 768
  freestanding 674
  gas 674
  hot air circulating 674
  indoor 674
  mantel 231,605,674
  masonry 674
  open end 674
  outdoor 73,316,668
  precast refractory 674
  radiant heat 674
Firestop 674
Fishing gear
  storage 130,266,630
Flashing 603,609,613,665,696
  chimney 674
Float,cartop swimming 247
Floating concrete 617,613
Floodlights 694,695
Floor
  how to lay 615,665
  level 608,685
  repair 608,685
  tile 606
  underlay 615
Flush Valve, toilet 675
Foam rubber, upholstery 623
Folding
  chair 56
  settee 55
  snack table 43
Footing 113,609,613,615,617,663,697
Footprints, giant 96
Form 613,617,668,697
Foundations 609,613,617,632,668,697
  waterproofing 632
Frames, picture 623,702
  window 159

Framing roof,floor,walls, new openings
501,502,603,609,613,631,632,
685,696,697,910
Free standing
room divider 658
Furniture
cabinet 634,658
colonial 761
contemporary 658
dollhouse 753
Furniture, repair 623
antiquing 623,761; caning 623
cane webbing 623
spring replacement 623
refinishing 623; reupholstery 623
Furring 609,605,615

Gable roof, studs 609,696,697
Garage
doors 86
one car 680
transform into housing 684
two car 663
two story 763
Garden, hotbed 611
tool house 51,89,649
trellis 304,607
Gates 315,941,607
Girders, covering 615,605
Glass sliding doors 613
Glazing 623
Glider, lawn 155,754
Gluing, complete guide 623
furniture 623
Golf cart 583
Grade level, establishing 632,668
Greenhouse 112,566,571,611
Grill, stall door 680,679
Grout 606,617,613,668
Guest house 84,684
Guide lines, laying out 632,668,697
Gun
cabinets 130,266,630
racks 574,630
Gutter 609,631,632,696
Gymnasium, outdoor 152,153,154

Hamster Cage751
Hardware
drapery 605, garage door 86
Headboard 126
Header 608,609,613,632,696,668
Hearth, prefabricated 674
Hi-Fi and radio 272,612
Hobby Horse 54
Home Workshop 677
Homes
country cottage 91
five-bedroom Cape Cod 514
guesthouse 84
hillside 103H—plans only
southwest corner 432,632
three-bedroom modern 502,513
three-bedroom ranch 501
two story garage apartment 763
two-bedroom ranch 910
valley house 103V—plans only
Hotbed, garden 611
Houseboat 676—26'
pontoons 600
House numbers, signs 801,607

Houses
retirement 632; bird 669
dog 28,751; doll 33,596,753
duck-in 725,751;
garden tools 51,89,649
green or hothouse 112,571; hog 13
lean-to storage 89; martin 669
play 148,649; poultry 14
rehabilitate 685; wiring 694
Hunter's cabinet 266,630
Hutch cabinet 270,761
rabbit 751

Indirect Lighting 694
Indoor Fireplace 674,231
Ironing board 615
Iron railings, repair 685

Jamb 605,697
Jig Saw, Pattern Asst. 102A,102B
with 10 full-size patterns 756

Kayak 317
Kitchen
blackboard 578
broom closet 156,634
buffet 138
cabinets 201,241-2-3-4-5-246,
608,658,634
counters 80,201,244,245,608,658
equipment templates 608,658
ironing board 615
knife rack 8; lighting 694
modernizing 608,605
planning 608; range installation 608
serving counter 80,243
sink enclosure 41,158
sink trap 682; traverse track 627
unit 3; utility closet 156
wall shelves 2,4,5,8
wall oven 608,658
work bench 573
Kite, Bermuda 314
Knick-Knack, see shelves

Lamps
modern table 98
outdoor colonial post 935,607
planter 541
repair 694
rooster, pin up 533
shadow box 557
Land selection 632
Lavatory enclosure 158,606
P trap 682
repair 675
Lawn or Patio
bench 57,307,325
chairs 32/39,55/56,311,314,
322R,548,754
chaise 78,169,312,324R,754
furniture repairs 623
glider 155,754
marker 102B
ornaments 9,81,96,304,102A,102B,672
settee 39,55
tables 17,22,75,323,554,577,754
Layout Stick
brick 668
concrete block 617
clapboard siding 609,684
tile 606
Lazy Susan 608,677

Lean-to tool shed 89,649,kennel,751
Level-Transit 668,697
Lighting 694
   built-in cornice,valance 694
   dark corner 557
   living room, draperies 627,694
   luminous ceiling, luminous 615,694
   wall sconce, candle 559
   walls, soffits, cove 694
Louver
   how to install 665,632
Lumber,chart 623
Magazine, rack 25,920,658,761
Mantel, fireplace 231,605,674
Martin House 669
Medicine Chest, repair 694
Message center, blackboard 313,578
Metal repairs
   roofing 696
Miter joint 605,609,664
Modern furniture 658
   also see furniture,bookcase,table
Modernization, attic 665,603,665
   bathroom 606,682
   basement 605,615
   kitchen 608,658
   lighting 694
   metal and wood cabinets 608,605
   refrigerator 605,608
Mortar—how to mix 668,617
   apply 609,613,617
Mullion or munion 613,609
Music Wall 612
Name Plates,Signs 102B,438,587,801,607
Night tables 343
Ornaments
   Christmas, see subject
   door chimes 561,677
   driveway 438
   sign & nameplate 102B,801,607
   table top 46
   wall-hanging 301,539,559,580,581,102
Outbuildings, see houses
Outdoor, lighting 694
Outlets, Electrical 694
Paneling,how to apply 605,609,615,665
Parakeet cage, 751
Partitions, see dividers 608,605,615
   658,665,773
Patio
   bench 57
   furniture, see lawn
   how to build 617,631,668
   how to screen 631
   paver tile 606,617
Peasant, shelf 2,4
   table 17
Pet projects
   cat shelter 724,751
   dog house 28,751
   dog kennel 751
   duck or chick-inn 725,751
   pet housing 751
   parakeet cage 751
   rabbit hutch 751
Picnic, see tables
Picture frames 97,623,702
Pipe rack, smoking 49,630
Pipes, covering 615
   repair 675

Pitch of roof 609,613,696,697
Planters
   indoors 46,82,102A,761
   lamp 541
Partition footings 632; post 617
   stable 680
   wall 501,502
Plaque, child's wall 102A/B
Plastic Laminate
   how to apply 608,658
   panels 631
Playground equipment
   see toys
Playhouses 148,649
Playroom bar 189,490,690,634
Play table 117
Plumb, how to 609,613,632,
   617,668,773
Plumbing
   continuous waste 682
   drain 682
   drum trap 682
   ferrule 682
   fittings 682
   fresh air inlet 682
   horizontal branch 682
   increaser 682
   kitchen sink trap 682
   lavatory 682
   plumbing wall 682
   repairs 675
   revent 682
   rough in 675,682
   slip joint 682
   soil pipe 682
   solder cup end 682
   spigot 682
   stack 682
   stack vent 682
   wall frame 632
   water pipe riser
Plunger
   toilet 675
Plywood
   how to panel 605
Pontoon 676,600
Pony
   book ends 102A,756
   rocker 53
Porch
   add-on 567,631
   build 613
   enclose 613
   sliding glass doors 613
Potholders Holder 102B, 756
Pram 77
Privacy partition 607,631,668
Quarry Tile
   606,617
Rabbit Hutch 751
Rack
   gun 630
   towel 29
Radio and Stereo
   bar 690
   cabinets 612,272
   how to build-in 612
Radiator enclosure 544,677
Rafters 609,613,631,632,663,696
Range installation 608

Record Cabinets 192,436,612
Refrigerator
  enclosure 608,658
  modernization 608,605
Reinforcing Rods, wire 617,668
Rehabilitate Buildings 685
Relax-a-Board 161
Remodeling 609,685
Repairs
  cane webbing 623
  concrete 617
  electrical 694
  furniture 623
  picture framing 623
  plumbing 675
  roofing 696
  tile 606
Ridge shingles 696
Rocker, pony ride 53
Rod, traverse 627
Roofing Repairs
  and Application 696
  asphalt
  repairs
  roll roofing
  safety harness 674,696,773
  scaffold 665,668,696
  slate
  wood
Room, add on 609,760
  dividers 128,658
  furniture 658
  roughing in 682
  wiring 694
Rowboats 77,85
Rush Weaving 623
Sabre Saw Pattern
  10 full-size projects 102A/B,756
Safety, see signs
Sailboat 194,248
Sandbox 20,77
Sawhorse-chest 672
Scaffold 665,668,680,696
Sconce, candle wall 559
Screed 617,631
Screen Enclosure 631,613
  how to make 631
Screw chart 658
Second floor apartment 773
Septic Tank 675
Service, center 243
  counter 80
Settee, see Lawn
Sewer Line 675
Sewing Cabinet 634
Sewing Tables 543
Shadow box 301,557
Sheathing, exterior 609,613,663,696
Shelves, wall 2,4,5,6,8,21,24,634,658,672
Shim 609,605
Shingles, asbestos 113,696,910
  roofing 432,609,663,696,910
Shoe rack 345
Shoe shine box 45
Shoe Equipment
  see workbench
Siding installation 609,663,696
Signs, nameplates 102B,801,607
Sink, repairs 675
  bar 201,608,658,690

counter installation 608
  enclosure 41,158
Skylight, how to install 665,696,773
Slant board 161
Slate Roofing 696
Slides, child's 63
Sliding door, wardrobes 139,634,658,773
Sliding stable door 679,680
Soil pipe 682
Solar heated greenhouse 611
Springs, furniture, cord bed 623
  retying, replacing, no-sag 623
Stable 679,680
Stairs, concrete 615,617
  how to build 603,615,617,665
  outside 763
Stall door 679,680
Star drill 679,680
Step Flashing 603,609,696
Stereo Wall 612
Stool, Tot's Step 353
Stilts 552
Stool, sill 605
Storage
  cabinets 3,24,159,634,242,608,658
  canned goods 770,608,623
  chest 37,962,634
  doll 159
  garden tool house 649
  headboard 126
  room divider 658
  sewing 634
  underbed 37
  undersink 41,158
  understair 634
  walls 612,658,634
  walls on casters 263
  wine storage 608,634,690
Storm windows 303
Stringer stair 603,665
Structural lighting 694
Studs 761,910,603
Studio bed, string 633,623,761
Subflooring 609
Sump Pump 615,617
Sundeck 631
Sunhouse 571
Surfboard or swimming float 247
Suspended ceiling 615
Swimming pool enclosure 631
Swings 152,155
Switch, wall 605,694

Tables
  bar 140, bridge 95, child's 117
  coffee 52,140,309,326,452
  colonial 94,761
  dining 94,95,137,554
  end 99,127,141
  folding 94,323
  lawn or terrace 17,75,326,554
  night table 343
  picnic 17,22,323,577
  round top 75,326
  serving, see coffee
  sewing 543
  TV 16,925
  wall attached 26,774
  workshop 15,568,573,576,672
Tape recorder, built-in 612

Telephone shelf 313
Termite Shield 609,632
Terrace 631,668
  table 75,326
Tile, see Ceramic 606
  asphalt 615
  counter 606
  how to lay 615
  vinyl 615
Toilet
  installation 682
  repairs 675
  replacement 675
Tool chests 71,576,634,672
Tommy gun, see toys
Tool houses
  expandable 51
  garage 113
  garden 51,649
  lean-to 89,649
  red barn 679
Tourist house 84
Towel rack 29
Toys
  airplane 70
  animals 79,83
  artists easel 555; boats 60,67
  carriage 59,773; chest 634
  circus group 48
  climbing, see playground
  clown 47; dollhouse 33,596,753
  furniture, see Children's
    dollhouse 753
  gas cart 583; glider 70
  gym, see playground
  hobby horse 54; machine gun 62
  how to build 771
  playground equipment
    climbing pole 154
    complete gym 152
    merry-go-round 733
    monkey bar 153
    sandbox 20,77
    slide 63
  playhouse 148,649
  playtable 117
  pony rocker 53; repairs 623
  stable 679
  step-stool 353, stilts 552
  storage 634,65; tommy gun 58
  toy chest 65; trainboard 190,677
  wagon 40; wheelbarrow 66
  workbench 15,672
Trainboard 190,677
Trap 675,682
  bathtub
  drum
  lavatory
  sink
  waste line
Traverse track 627
Tree well 668
Trellis 305,607
Trim, apply 615
Trophy cabinet 630
TV table 16
Under bed storage 634,761
Understair storage 634
Upholstery, repair 623
Utility closet 156,634

Valance
  bookcase 271
  indirect lighting 157,694
  window 1,27,30,550,627
Valley Flashing 696
Vanity 658
  bathroom 606
Veneer, brick 668
Wall decorations 97,159M,539,
  580,581,702, see ornaments
Wall
  framing 663,608
  oven 608,658
  paneling 605
  plaque, child's 102A/B
  remove 608
  retaining 668
  shelves, see shelves
  storage 634
  switch 694
  waterproof 615
  wiring 694
Walks, brick 668
Wardrobe 139,193,263,634,658
Washers
  faucet 675
  sizes 675
Water pipe riser 682
Water Shut Off
  valve 675
Waterproofing 617
Weathervane 524,588,589
Webbing, furniture 623
Wheelbarrow 66
Wind braces 632
Window
  bookcase 271
  bow, picture, installation 609
  framing 159
  glazing 613,623
  greenhouse 566,611
  how to install 609
  how to move 608
  how to repair window 685
  storm 303
  valance 1,27,30,550,627,694
Wiring, electric 615,694
Wood conversion chart 613
Wood shingles 696
Workbench 568,672,677
Workshop 677
Worktable 573,672
Wren house 11,111,102B,669,756